PUBLISH

TAKE CHARGE OF YOUR AUTHOR CAREER

PUBLISH

TAKE CHARGE OF YOUR AUTHOR CAREER

GRETA BORIS &
MEGAN HASKELL

O.C. Writers Press

www.OCWriters.network/publish

Ordering Information:
Quantity sales. Special discounts are available on quantity purchases by corporations, associations, and others. For details, contact the publisher at the address above.

Cover design by Michelle Fairbanks

Edited by Kimberly Peticolas

Interior format by Kimberly Peticolas

Print ISBN 978-0-9994354-2-7

ePub ISBN 978-0-9994354-3-4

Dedicated to DeAnna Cameron and the O.C. Writers Community for challenging and inspiring us to write this book.

Contents

Foreword

In 2010, e-books slammed into the publishing world and caused an earthquake of epic proportions. The dam erected by the big New York publishing houses cracked in the upheaval, and a flood of self-published books hit the marketplace. Whether this was a disaster or a blessing is still being sorted out. One thing is certain—the world of publishing was forever altered.

We've heard it said that this is the best time in history to be an author. We've also heard it's the worst. We believe it's up to you which is true. There are more options, but options are only an advantage if you're willing to do the research to understand their benefits and challenges. Along with the expansion of legitimate independent and boutique publishers, came a myriad of people ready to take advantage of the new chinks in the system.

Thousands of unedited, unprofessional novels fail on the internet every year. Vanity presses and scam publicity companies promising unrealistic results advertise to these disappointed writers and others who want to avoid the same disappointment. But there are many excellent service providers available as well.

In this book, we endeavor to help you find your way through the rubble, to sort through the good, the bad, and the just plain ugly in today's publishing world, and to build an author career that fits your personality, lifestyle, and project. Greta Boris will tackle the two traditional paths, agented and boutique, while Megan Haskell guides you through the independent journey.

But first: the pros and cons of each.

Traditional Agented Path:

Many publishing houses, large and small, only accept manuscripts submitted by a literary agent. You, as an author, can't send them your work without an invitation. If you plan to take this route—pitch to agents, hope one accepts you, then pray he or she is able to sell your manuscript to a publisher—patience is essential. This is the longest path to publication, but it can have terrific rewards.

Agents can help shape a career. They have an understanding of the industry and connections you as an author don't. They can open the door to large publishing houses which often give authors more exposure, distribution in bookstores and libraries, cover blurbs by recognized authors and, of course, prestige.

On the negative side of this publishing route are time and low royalties. It can take a long time to find an agent, and then that agent has to sell your book. The royalty split for a new writer with a bigger house is somewhere in the vicinity of ten percent, and you must share that ten percent with your agent.

Traditional Boutique Path:

Another publishing option is to pitch directly to one of the many smaller boutique houses that don't require an agent as a go-between. Often these publishers are either new and don't have the track record to tempt agents, or they are genre specific—for instance, they only publish cozy mysteries, or romance, or they are an e-book only press.

Boutique publishers are not to be confused with "vanity" presses, or companies you hire to help you publish your work. Boutique publishing houses go through the same selection process as their larger counterparts, but publish a smaller number of titles each year.

The advantages to working with a boutique press are: you often don't need an agent, but can query directly; you generally have input on at least some of the publishing decisions; your royalty cut is higher; and they have more invested in you, so work more closely with you to market your books. If the publisher takes author submissions because they are new, and they accept you, you may be first in the door of what will one day be a prestigious press.

The disadvantages are: they don't have the reach of the bigger houses, probably won't be able to sell as many books to large bookstores, and don't carry the same status. Also, there is a greater risk they will go out of business, which puts the onus on you to do your research.

Independent Publishing Path:

These days successful indie authors, and there are many, act as their own publishing house. They do all the things a traditional press does except acquisitions, which means the limits of the independent author correspond to their own network and ability to think and act like an entrepreneur. For example, you'll need to find and hire your own team—editors, cover designers, formatters, etc.—and you'll make every decision on the marketing of your book, from retail price to advertising and promotions.

On the plus side, your hard work could be well rewarded. You keep all the royalties from the sale of a book (retail price less a percentage paid to the bookseller), which means you can make more money selling fewer books. You can also act faster than the traditional presses, moving with the market and changing your plans as new technologies and new opportunities arise. If you're a fast writer, this means you can successfully publish multiple titles in a single year, rather than waiting on a traditional press's marketing calendar.

The major drawback is time and money. Once your book is ready for publication, you must do your own launch, find reviewers, plan your marketing . . . the list goes on. Putting all of that together will take time away from writing your next book, and requires a different, more logical, left-brain mindset. Plus, there are start-up costs to self-publishing. You must invest in yourself and your project to produce a viable product that readers will want to buy.

Another drawback for some authors is that despite the improved perception of self-publishing in recent years, there can still at times be a stigma against independently published authors from the traditional market. Some major book awards are limited to traditionally published titles, and it can be extremely difficult, if not impossible, to get your books into major bookstore chains or libraries. If your goals involve major accolades and becoming a household name, self-publishing might not be the best path for you.

In the end, to be a successful indie author you must treat your art as a business and plan for a long career. Done right, you could end up more financially successful than your traditional counterparts.

Hybrid Publishing

Whichever path to publication you pursue, most successful authors will tell you marketing is a part of every writer's life these days. The difference is whether you are in full control, or work with a team. Every publishing house has different policies when it comes to marketing, some favorable, some not so favorable. Authors are also realizing they may have different goals for different projects, or the manuscript itself might be better suited for one publication path over another. Enter the hybrid author.

Publishing is no longer a one-size fits all model. There are authors who are both traditionally published and self-published. There are small presses that act like co-ops, where each author contributes their skills to the collective group of projects in publication. Other companies will offer paid services on an a la carte menu. You can even find presses that will purchase "print-only" rights, meaning the author will self-publish the e-book while the press publishes and markets the paperback.

For the purposes of this book, we're not going to focus on these infinite combinations, but keep in mind that while you may choose to pursue traditional publishing with your current work in progress, you might change your mind for the next project, or the one after that.

NAVIGATING "*PUBLISH*"

We've divided this book into four primary sections, each focused on a different aspect of the writing and publishing game. We begin with choosing your path and finding your publishing team in Section One. In Section Two, we'll talk about goal setting and project management, both critical to sticking with the process and achieving a positive result. Section Three is all about staying focused, developing your career, and finding your audience. Last, we'll tackle book launches and some basic marketing techniques in Section Four.

Before we get into all that, however, take the Publishing Personality Quiz on the next page and discover which path you're best cut out for. You might be surprised at the result.

Find the Publishing Personality Quiz answers by turning to page 121.

What's Your Publishing Personality?

1. How do you manage your personal finances?
   a. I have overdraft protection
   b. I have a detailed budget and monitor revenues and expenses
   c. I balance my bank accounts occasionally
2. What's your ideal production schedule?
   a. More than two books a year.
   b. At least one book every two years.
   c. At least one book a year.
3. How do you envision your role in the editorial process?
   a. I see my editor as a collaborator and want to find mutual agreement.
   b. I value critique but see myself as the final decision maker.
   c. I might not like it, but understand I will have to make changes to see my book in print.
4. How do you feel about marketing?
   a. I want time to experiment and explore the marketing options that best fit me.
   b. I want to work with a team to promote both myself and others.
   c. I want to build my author platform before publication and am willing to promote myself assertively.
5. How willing are you to give up control of your cover design?
   a. Not at all.
   b. Completely.
   c. Would like some input.
6. What kind of financial investment are you ready to make in your work?
   a. I have some money to invest, and am looking for a financial partner.
   b. I don't plan to invest. I want to sell my writing for a set fee.
   c. I'm willing to spend money now with an expectation of a long-term return on investment.

SECTION 1

ReCON

"I would advise anyone who aspires to a writing career that before developing his talent he would be wise to develop a thick hide."

—Harper Lee, Writer's Digest 1961

No man is an island. Most writers consider themselves to be introverts, lone wolves, the Jack Reachers of the world, but in actuality you need a team if you're going to survive in the publishing wilds. You need to **ReCON**.

Re - Research your options

C - Connect

O - Overcome rejection and criticism

N - Nice guys finish first

In this section you'll learn to identify the team members you need for your particular publishing path, be they agents, independent editors, publishers, or graphic designers. You'll be provided with best practices for finding and connecting with those individuals and some tips on how to create a successful working relationship once you do. We've laid out the information by pathway. Greta will be your traditional guide, and Megan will lead you down the road to independent publishing.

CHAPTER 1

RESEARCH YOUR OPTIONS

Hopefully by now you've taken the Publishing Personality test and have an idea which path to publication you plan to pursue: Traditional Agented, Traditional Boutique, or Independent. Are you still considering more than one? Not to worry. We'll help you explore all your options.

TRADITIONAL AGENTED

A good literary agent can be worth their weight in gold. Literary agents agree to represent an author's work in exchange for a percentage of the royalties made when that work is published. Never work with an agent who wants to charge you up front. A genuine agent is in a commission sales position. If they can't sell your book to a publisher, they won't make money. If they sell it, but the publisher doesn't market it well, they won't make money. It's the risk they take on when they sign up for the job.

This is why agents are so difficult to obtain. They can't afford to spend time on a book they don't believe will sell well. They can be very valuable players to have on your side. They have expertise and industry connections you don't have. They can shape a career and help you find your way as an author. It's a good idea for all aspiring authors, whatever path they choose for publication, to have a literary agent review their work. They understand the market probably better than any other industry professional.

The first time I met with an agent I had no idea what I was doing. I sent an early submission into the Southern California Writers Conference in Irvine. Writers' conferences are a wonderful way to learn about the publishing industry. I heartily recommend attending any that are in your area.

An early submission program is offered by some conferences for an additional fee. I paid fifty dollars, sent ten pages of my manuscript to an agent who was planning to attend, and received a fifteen-minute appointment in which she agreed to review my work with me. I met with Jennifer Azantian who had just started her own agency.

Prior to writing fiction, my background was nonfiction: a self-help book, magazine articles, and marketing copy. In all those disciplines, edgy and unique ways of expressing concepts is not only accepted, it's expected. This is my way of explaining why I thought describing my novel as "cozy horror" was a good idea. It wasn't.

Jennifer pointed out, very kindly, while I could call my genre anything I wanted on my own website, there were certain industry standards and "cozy horror" wasn't one of them. In her estimation, my book was a thriller with supernatural elements.

Having said all that, a bad agent is worse than no agent. They can stall a career. It can take a good agent a year, or even longer, to sell your book. A bad agent may never try, or may promote your story to the wrong market. Two years later you have no publishing deal and no agent, and you're back to square one. The moral of that story is: When seeking representation, do your research.

A Note on the Importance of Genre

New fiction writers often don't understand the nuances of their chosen genre. When you ask them what they're writing they launch into a long description of the plot of their story. Most people only want to hear the genre and logline. There's information about how to tease a logline out of your story in Chapter Two, but let's look at genre here.

You probably have some idea of what you're writing. You know if it's mystery/thriller, science fiction/fantasy, romance, or general fiction. If these definitions are new to you, I suggest you do an internet search and read up on the basics before you dive into the project below.

Once you know the broad genre your book fits within, it's time to drill down further. If you're writing a thriller for instance, is it geo-political, psychological, or a police procedural? Think about books you've read that are similar to yours and look them up on Amazon. How are they defined there?

Once you know the subgenre of your story, do a search to discover the titles that have won awards or been bestsellers within that category within the past two or three years. Next step is to head to the library with that list in hand. Put as many of those books as you can find on a table, take a legal pad and make a list of the following:

Titles: Are there any similarities in the titles? Are they long? Short? One Word? Are there common words or themes?

Length: How many pages do they have? How many chapters? Are the chapters long or short?

Point of View (POV): Is it written in first person? Third person close? Third person distant? How many POV characters are there?

Style: How long are the sentences? What kind of language is used? How much white space is on the page? How much descriptive language? How much dialogue?

Plot: What are there common themes in these titles?

Opening Hook: How does the author hook you into the story? How does the book start?

Use this information to polish your manuscript and prepare your pitch. If you're thinking about writing a book series, you might want to jump ahead to Chapter Twelve where that topic is addressed, then come back. The more you understand the publishing industry and where your story fits, the more likely an agent or editor will take you seriously.

Where Do You Find Agents?

- Agent Query (http://Agentquery.com)
- Publisher's Marketplace (www.publishersmarketplace.com)
- Querytracker (http://querytracker.net)

- *Writer's Market*—a new edition comes out every year. It's generally in the library, or can be purchased in bookstores or online.

In all the above resources, you'll find lists of agents open to submissions and the genres those agents are looking for. But none of them will tell you much about the agent's ability.

A Few Ways to Investigate Agents Are:

- Do an internet search on the agents who look interesting to you. Find authors those agents represent. Their authors should be listed on their websites. How are their authors doing? Do the authors mention the agent in the acknowledgment section of their books?
- Ask other authors in your genre about their agents, or other agents they may know about.
- Follow agents on social media

I used to follow literary agents on Twitter to see the kinds of things they tweeted. Some were so snarky I chose not to pitch to them.

Traditional Boutique

A traditional boutique press, or a small press, should do essentially all the same things a larger press will do for you. The biggest differences are: often they're open to submissions from authors who don't have agents, especially when the press is new; they offer a higher royalty percentage; they don't have the connections, prestige, or budgets of their larger counterparts.

I was offered a contract from a boutique press a few years ago. I popped the champagne bottle, did a jig, and rejoiced.

The next day, I checked them out. Their website and their Facebook page set off alarm bells in me. I didn't like their covers. There were typos in their website copy. Their books had few, or poor, Amazon reviews.

I friended one of their authors on Facebook. She had books published with a variety of publishers. When she accepted my request I messaged her and asked about her experience with this press. She said she did one book with them and that was enough for her. I turned down that contract.

Because the query process (this is covered in Chapter Two) is so difficult and writers receive so many rejections, the temptation is to jump at the first "yes" that comes. But just as a bad agent is worse than no agent, a bad publisher is worse than no publisher.

Once you sign that contract, your story is in their hands. If they hire a poor editor, slap on an unprofessional cover, and never do more than tweet about your book launch it reflects on you. Most readers don't care who publishes a book. They don't even notice. But your name is in bold letters on the front cover.

Try approaching the pursuit of a boutique press the way you might approach house hunting. Sit down and make lists. First, write down the things you have to have, the non-negotiables. For me, this included print and digital books. I wanted to see my work in bookstores. Small independent stores were fine, but the publisher had to have bookstore connections. Their books must be well edited and the covers professional. The author stable must be one I'd be happy to be part of. Their books must have more reviews than I could get on my own.

Next, write down things you hope for, but aren't deal breakers. This list for me included a marketing manager and some input in cover design and book pricing. Finally, make your this-would-be-amazing list. On mine, I had a company that would attempt to sell subsidiary rights and would enter my titles in book award contests. I got everything I'd hoped for when I found my publisher, including my this-would-be-amazing list. So can you, but it will take research and patience.

Places to look for a boutique press:

- Google search "Publishers open to un-agented submissions."
- https://Duotrope.com is a website that lists thousands of publishing companies open to un-agented submissions. They include a lot of short form submission sites (poetry, articles, short stories) but they include some novel length publishing houses as well.
- Publisher's Marketplace (www.publishersmarketplace.com)
- *Writer's Market*—a new edition comes out every year. It's generally in the library, or can be purchased in bookstores or online.

INDEPENDENT:

The indie path is not as straightforward as you might think. Indie authors need to do research, create contracts, and beware the traps of the vanity presses. Which means that while independent publishing is a faster path to market than the traditional options, the publishing process still takes time, especially the first time. In fact, my first book took five months to produce, from the time I hired my editor until I hit publish.

The First Step on Your Independent Journey: Find Your Team.

Developmental Editor ($500 – $2k+):

A developmental editor is someone you hire to critique your overall story. This person should tell you if your plot has holes, your pacing is too fast (or too slow), your dialogue is flat, and whether or not your characters are believable. This is usually an early edit—sometimes even during the outlining phase—and revisions can involve major rewrites.

Copyeditor and Proofreader ($500 – $2k+):

A copyeditor provides line-by-line feedback on spelling, grammar, punctuation, and the elements of style. A proofreader reviews the final formatted manuscript for any remaining mistakes, which could be spelling or grammar, but might also be page layout and design. Sometimes you only need to hire one person to fill this role, sometimes you need two different people. It depends on the editor, your project, and your writing style.

Cover Designer ($50 – $1k+):

The cover designer is the graphic artist who creates the cover for your book. In some cases, this is a single person or company, who will use stock photography and photo-manipulation software (like Photoshop) to design both the images and text. In other cases, you might consider hiring an illustrator to design the imagery, and a typographer to add the text. Obviously, the more people you hire, and the more custom the cover, the higher the cost. On the cheaper side, you can look for pre-made covers with customizable text for your book.

Fair warning: pre-made covers often look pre-made. That is to say, they're not particularly unique or creative, and might not be the best for your particular project. I also strongly recommend you avoid designing the cover yourself unless you have a solid background in graphic design or are willing to spend a significant amount of time learning how to use Photoshop.

Print & E-book Formatter ($20 – $500):

Formatters will create the layout of the interior text of your book. You can hire them to create your paperback (a pdf file), your e-book (a mobi file for Kindle, and an ePub for everyone else), or both. Formatters are generally able to produce a higher quality product with customized design elements than you could produce using basic html formatting or available software products. That said, many writers choose to save money by learning the basics of formatting, especially for novels.

Publicity or Book Launch Strategist ($20 – $500+):

There are plenty of people who will try to sell you promotion and book launch services. Some of these are legitimate, and can help increase your visibility in the market. Others will convince you that they can turn you into an overnight best-seller, only to run away with the cash. Think critically and ask for author referrals before you hire anyone to promote your book.

Beta Readers (Typically $0 . . . breathe a sigh of relief):

Keep reading for more on beta readers.

I hear your thoughts whirling as you read this list and add up the possible costs of becoming an independent author. I understand.

#1 Expense for an Indie Author: Editing

Editors are expensive. Editing is the number one cost in producing a high-quality book, but it's also the only one that everyone needs. And I mean *everyone*.

As the author, your book is your baby. To you, your baby is beautiful, perfect. You're so enamored with it you can't see its flaws. But unlike an actual baby, people won't hesitate to judge it in the real world. A book is fair game for tough reviews and criticism. In fact, since you're asking people to pay money to read your work, it's only natural that they want the best for their money.

As an independent author, you're going to want to cut costs. You might think that you don't need an editor, that you're tough enough on yourself that you can read the book objectively. Ninety-nine percent of the time, you're wrong. You need at least one extra pair of eyes on your manuscript to find those flaws you can't see.

In truth, the brain is a magnificent liar. Studies have shown that the brain will overlook errors while reading, because it knows what you're trying to say. *You* understand your story, so you are physically unable to see or comprehend the mistakes in the text. An external perspective is essential to making sure your message is clear, your prose is coherent, and your grammar is sound.

So you need an editor. At least one person to review your manuscript and check for plot holes, typos, or other errors. But cost is definitely a factor for the indie author. When strapped for cash, there are some ways to mitigate your expenses. For example, you may be able to do without a developmental editor if you've utilized Beta Readers well.

Beta Readers: Who They Are and What They Do

What are Beta Readers? These are individuals—often other writers or fans—who will read your work and give you critical feedback. Sometimes they do it in exchange for your critique on their work. Sometimes it's just because they love you and your stories.

After I finished the first draft of what would become my first published novel, I was excited. Thrilled! For the first time, I had a finished manuscript I truly believed in. Problem was, no one else had read it, and as good as I felt about it, I knew that wasn't good enough. Not yet. I needed someone to help me find the weaknesses in the story, everything from overall structure to dialogue and setting. I couldn't afford a developmental editor, so where could I find someone to help?

At the time, I wasn't connected to the writing community. But when I began talking to people, it turned out I knew more writers than I realized. A good friend had been a screenwriter in a prior career, and her sister and former co-writer was working on a fantasy novel. My friend put us in touch, and pretty soon we were meeting every month, swapping chapters, and slowly but surely improving our craft. Over the course of nine months, we polished and perfected until I was confident in the quality of the story and ready to show the book to the wider world.

What *aren't* beta readers? People who want to boost your ego. Your mom is probably not a good choice. You *must* find beta readers who won't hold back, who have no fear of hurting your feelings, or making you angry, *especially* if you're not planning to hire a developmental editor.

That's why it was brilliant that my critique partner was the sister of my friend. There was enough distance between us that we weren't afraid to give honest opinions, but because we still had someone in common (and met in person), we made sure our critiques were constructive.

Find Ways to Save Cash and Still Get What You Need

Now take that same concept and look at the other service providers. Ask yourself what are your personal skills? Can you save a bit of money by doing the work yourself? What *can't* you do, and still produce a professional product?

I'm not a visual artist. I have zero experience in Photoshop. Therefore, if I want a professional product, I have to hire my cover artist. BUT, I did figure out how to do my own formatting in Scrivener, a word processing software designed specifically for long-form writers. It might not have the artistic flair of some books, but still looks like a high-quality, professionally produced book.

There are other ways to save cash as well. Can you trade services? For example, if you're great with website design, maybe you can update your artist's website. Or, if you're a CPA, does your editor need her taxes done?

You're a writer. Be creative. Find ways to get the services you need. Don't skimp just because you don't have the cash.

Finding Service Providers

A great place to start the process of finding service providers is in your own writing community. If you don't have one, ask around. You might be surprised whom you're connected to. There are also fantastic groups online made up of indie authors who are willing to share. Many groups publish lists of recommended freelance editors, cover designers, formatters—everyone you need to produce a quality book. Ask questions of other authors, especially in your genre.

Here Are a Few Great Places to Look:

- Referrals from other authors
- K-Boards (https://www.kboards.com): This is a discussion board website for authors and readers alike. There is a wealth of information in the forums. They also include a "Yellow Pages" for author service providers. If you haven't yet joined, you should definitely look into it.
- Facebook Groups (See Appendix for recommendations)
- Google Search
- Conferences
- Other Networking

Now you know whom you need to find, but how do you connect with them?

Chapter 2

Connect

Once you've decided whom you want to hire, it's time to reach out and determine if they're truly right for you and your project. Be they agents, small presses, or freelance service providers, you shouldn't necessarily sign with the first person who likes your work. In this chapter, you'll learn where to make connections, the basics of querying, and how to reach out as a professional author.

From this chapter forward, we are dropping the distinction between Traditional Agented and Traditional Boutique publishing because the two paths now merge. The query process for a traditional deal is the same whether you're pitching your book to an agent or to an editor at a smaller house.

Traditional Publishing

An agent I met at a conference a few years back told me she received on average a thousand submissions a month. Out of that number she took on about five books. Attempting to get an agent or a small press without an introduction is a bit like winning the lottery. Some people do it, but I suggest hedging your bets.

Ask anyone in sales—a warm lead beats a cold one any day of the week. If an agent or acquisition editor can put a face on a query letter, he or she is much more likely to read it. In this first stage of the game, that's your goal. Later we'll worry about fine-tuning your sales pitch, but for now, you just want to make some contacts.

How do you meet a real person? Sometimes you need to stalk the agent or publisher of your dreams on social media to find out where they hang out. Another method is to look at events you can add to your calendar and research the industry professionals who will be attending. Are any of them people you'd be interested in working with? If so, sign up.

Places to Make Connections:

- Conferences: early submissions, meet and greet events, rogue read and critiques, author idol contests
- Contests and award competitions: sometimes the prize is representation, and if not, an award still looks great in a query letter
- Twitter Pitches: both agents and acquisition editors peruse Twitter pitches
- An introduction from another author

I found my publisher through a Twitter Pitch. Here's how they work: Someone, usually another author, contacts a list of editors and agents and asks them if they'll agree to check a certain hashtag on a certain day during certain hours. Writers tweet their book descriptions using the event hashtag. (Which uses up some of your 140 characters, by the way.) The industry professionals then hit the like button on your tweet if they want you to send them a full query.

Each contest has its own rules about how many tweets you can send and when you can send them, but every one I've seen recommends you change your pitch each time. This gives you a chance to see which bait attracts the most fish and, in turn, helps you write the logline for your query letter. (See *How to Tease a Logline Out of Your Story* below.) A logline is an essential ingredient in any query or book proposal and later can be used to market your published book.

A query letter is like a résumé for a fiction book. A book proposal has the same function for a nonfiction book. There are things that should be included and things that shouldn't in each. Each has a particular format and writing them is an art unto itself.

While you're researching your dream team, or waiting for the next conference or Twitter Pitch, get started on your query letter or your book proposal. Don't wait until you have a hot prospect. These letters are almost as difficult to write as your book was. Some think they're more difficult. If you've had the chance to make a personal contact, make sure to act on it quickly. Don't forget—agents and editors receive so many submissions, they will forget all about you if you dawdle around for weeks with your letter.

How to Tease a Logline Out of Your Story

There are entire classes taught on the subject of writing a logline, but Twitter pitches are a great place to start.

When writing a Twitter pitch, you should include the protagonist's career or role, what they want, the struggle they must overcome to get it and, possibly, the setting. It's a challenge to boil all that down into 140 characters minus the hashtag, but it's great practice. When you get good at it, writing a logline, which allows you to use two entire sentences to describe your story, feels like a luxury.

Step 1: Answer These Questions

- Who is my story about? I don't want her name. I want her occupation, her place in life, why you chose her as your protagonist.
- What does he want that he doesn't have? If he doesn't want something that seems unattainable, you don't have a story.
- What's stopping her from getting it? Conflict. Gotta have it.
- Where does the story take place? This is optional. For some stories setting is really important. For others, not so much.

Example:

Here's how I answered those questions from my book, *A Margin of Lust*.

- An ambitious real estate agent
- To sell the expensive listing she just acquired, success, prestige
- Someone keeps sabotaging the sale
- Laguna Beach, Orange County, California

Step 2.: Answer the Questions in One or Two Sentences

There are a lot of ways I could go with my information. Here are a few:

- *Every time an ambitious real estate agent puts her Laguna Beach, ocean view listing on the market, something goes horribly wrong.* (131 characters)
- *An ambitious real estate agent lands a multi-million dollar listing, and winds up in a battle with a mysterious force bent on sabotaging the sale.* (148 characters)
- *An O.C. Realtor has two big fears: claustrophobia and being buried in suburban obscurity. When she finds the body of a fellow agent she ought to develop a third. Someone's stalking her.* (187 characters)

How do you know which bait is best?

This is where Twitter Pitches come in. What better way to test your logline than on a day where you're free to send 140 character descriptions of your novel out at regular intervals to industry professionals?

Here's the pitch that got me five requests for full queries, two requests for full manuscripts and ultimately a contract: A real estate agent's new Laguna Beach listing is perfect, except for the body upstairs and what's hidden in the cellar.

Why this one? I don't know. It's not my favorite. I like all that suburban obscurity stuff better. But if bread balls catch more fish than night crawlers, what are you going to use?

You can use your winning Twitter pitch as the logline for your query letter with a few modifications. Now that you're no longer restricted to 130 – 135 characters, it almost seems easy. Here is how mine morphed: An ambitious real estate agent's multi-million dollar, Laguna Beach, ocean view listing would be perfect if it wasn't for the body in an upstairs bedroom and the secret hidden in the cellar.

I was able to use some of my favorite phrases in the longer description of the story and for the final book description that's now on my website.

Anatomy of a Fiction Query Letter

There are many websites and online courses focused solely on how to write a good query letter. We've included a few in the resources section of this book. I suggest looking into the free information available as well, but here are the basics.

- Tailor your letter to the individual you're pitching. Say something personal in the introduction.
- Follow the guidelines on the website *exactly*.
- Write a good logline, or hook (See the above Breakout Box).
- Let him or her know length, genre, and possible comparison authors.
- Write a short (three paragraph at most) synopsis.
- Write a short (one paragraph) bio of pertinent information (Not where you were born, went to school, etc . . . unless it impacts your work).
- Never send an attachment unless it's specifically requested.
- Be professional.

The Nonfiction Book Proposal:

When writing a book proposal for a nonfiction book, you will follow the above steps with a few differences. Rather than a synopsis of plot and characters when writing your summary, an outline in the form of chapter headings and descriptions is often sufficient.

The biography section is much more important when pitching a nonfiction book. You need to focus on the market you're writing for, what qualifies you to write the book, your author platform, and marketing strategies.

Another important distinction between a book proposal and a fiction query letter is when pitching nonfiction you don't have to have a completed manuscript. When pitching fiction, your manuscript must be complete and as polished as you can make it.

Tracking Your Queries

Your next step is to make a spreadsheet to track your queries. Set it up with columns for name, company, the date you pitched, what you sent, the date you can expect a response, and the response. You will forget whom you sent what if you don't, which is both unprofessional and embarrassing. A sample spreadsheet is included in the appendix.

Independent Publishing

Before you start connecting with the service providers you identified in Chapter One, you're going to need a query letter. Yes, indies need them too. Admittedly they're not the same as the letters to agents or publishing houses, but you do need a professional, quality email to entice service providers. Many of them, especially the good ones, are selective about their projects. It's important to put your best foot forward.

The Indie Process:

Submission Guidelines: Find the website of each service provider you might want to hire, and look for specific submission guidelines. Follow the instructions *exactly*. Some service providers may want an email, others use a submission form. Some may want a specific list of information, others leave it open ended. Double and triple check before hitting send.

References: Understand the service provider's portfolio and references. For example, editors should have a list of clients they've worked with and perhaps testimonials for the quality of their work. Cover artists should have an online gallery of their designs. Look for freelancers who are experienced in your genre. A cover designer who specializes in thrillers might not be the best choice for nonfiction. Do your due diligence, and verify their claims before giving them any money.

The Email: When writing an email to a potential contractor, make sure you introduce yourself, share why you're contacting them, who referred you (if you have a referral) and what drew your attention to their work, plus a brief (two to three sentences) synopsis of your project. If they don't have submission guidelines on their website, ask if they're taking new clients, and what information they require to evaluate the project.

Hiring an Editor: Before paying a thousand dollars for a full edit of your manuscript, request a test edit. Many editors will offer special pricing to review a small sample of your work—usually the first chapter, or up to the first fifty pages. The test edit will give you a good idea of the quality of their work and whether you enjoy working with them. If they don't list it on their website, make sure to ask.

Contracts: Ask to review the service provider's standard contract early in the connection phase. It doesn't always have to be a formal document, but there should be clear and detailed terms, including project start dates, end dates, payment schedules, and cancellation terms. Make sure the terms are agreeable and sign the contract before starting work.

Author Beware

My good friend and fellow author, Jeffrey J. Michaels, likes to say, "There are more people making money on writers, than writers making money on writing." Unfortunately, I tend to agree.

There are a lot of predatory people hunting for uninformed writers. There are companies that will offer to publish your book for a mere ten thousand dollars, then do nothing more than give you an inexperienced editor and stock cover design. There are promotion companies that will—for just two hundred dollars—tweet your book five times a day for a week to their hundred thousand followers who may or may not be interested in reading anything, let alone buying your book.

Don't be afraid to ask questions and think critically about the services you're hiring. Consider the quality of your end product and your potential return on investment. How many books do you have to sell just to break even? Don't be a sucker and jump at every opportunity that's presented to you.

CHAPTER 3

OVERCOME REJECTION AND CRITICISM

Our joint feeling about criticism is: it's best to pull off the Band Aid. If you've been a part of a critique group, or utilized beta readers, you're smart. Regardless of which path to publication you're pursuing, get as much criticism as you can before exposing your work to industry professionals.

TRADITIONAL PUBLISHING

When a writer begins the query process they *will be* rejected—not maybe, possibly, or sometimes. It's a universal experience. There's a remote possibility one lucky writer in a million will snag a contract on the first go round, but I've never met one. Unless your father owns a publishing company or your mother is a celebrity, it's a safe bet when you begin to shop your manuscript around, you're going to hear the big N-O more than once.

Before I found my publisher, I pitched around seventy-five agents and editors. I know that sounds like a lot, but it's not that many in the grand scheme of things. Sometimes it was painful, but it was an education. Rejection teaches you a lot about the industry. You'll meet successful agents you'd never be able to work with even if they wanted to sign you. You'll investigate reputable publishing houses where you'd be miserable. The query process will help you fine-tune your wish list.

If every rejection throws you into despair, you'll never find success. Too many writers give up on the query process and either self-publish (not as an author-entrepreneur which is a serious and professional undertaking, but alone, without resources, and desperate) or walk away. I made it my mission to learn from every rejection. I even got to the point where I graded them. Bad rejections were form letters and silences. Better rejection letters were personal. The best rejections told me what was wrong with the work so I could improve.

Silence and Form Letters

When you receive a form letter, it means the person you pitched was so disinterested, or busy, or overwhelmed, he or she didn't read it. In my first year of pitching, these were about all I got.

What form letters *do* tell you:

- You pitched the wrong person.
- It was bad timing.
- Your query letter or book proposal needs help.
- They weren't looking for what you wrote.

What form letters *don't* tell you:

- Your writing is bad (although it may be).
- Your book premise is bad (although it may be).
- You're an abject failure (you're not).

After every ten to fifteen rejections, re-read your query and opening pages, or book proposal with a critical eye. Ask others for input. What can you change to make it better? Tweak, revise, and resend.

Personal Rejections

At some point, I began to get personal rejections in which an agent or editor told me what they liked and what they didn't like. Some of these were incredibly painful. Sometimes I cried. But then I wiped my eyes, recognized I'd moved up the ladder a few rungs and tried to learn from the experience.

What personal rejections tell you:

- You're getting closer.
- You may consider revising based on what they said.
- You may hone in on the type of person you're pitching.
- Sometimes your letter is the problem.

An editor from a boutique press I really wanted to publish with once sent me a long letter explaining why he wouldn't buy my manuscript. One of his criticisms was my protagonist wasn't likeable. All my beta readers had found my main character very likeable. In fact, one of the critiques I'd received was that she was too nice!

I wanted to call that editor up and tell him how wrong he was. My protagonist was a doll, a gem. He'd completely misunderstood her. Then I had an epiphany. He only had the first ten pages of the manuscript and my synopsis. One or both were at fault.

My synopsis was the culprit. In my attempt to prove my character had an emotional arc, was deep and complex, I'd exaggerated her flaws. After I rewrote the query letter, I began getting requests for full manuscripts.

The rejections really got interesting then. One editor gave me an outline of what she found wrong with my novel and said if I'd be willing to revise my story based on her critique, she'd take another look at it.

What revise and resubmit requests tell you:

- Your premise is strong.
- Your writing is strong.
- If you want to work with this editor or agent, this is an opportunity.

I did revise and resubmit, but found another publisher before that editor ever responded. I was very grateful for her critique, however. I believe it's the reason I eventually signed a contract even though it wasn't with her. She helped me write a better book—a book that sold.

Independent Publishing

The most important thing for an indie author to keep in mind is patience. Don't rush to publication just because you can. You can't avoid criticism and rejection by avoiding the traditional pitching process; they're part of the writer's experience. Although every writer's journey is unique, I've never met a single one who didn't have a negative review, a nasty critique, or a heartbreaking disappointment. It's how you deal with it that matters.

My Path to Publication

I was a hobbyist writer for many years, just passing the time on the train as I commuted to work. When I eventually decided I wanted to try my hand at writing a novel, it took me four years and several false starts to finish that first manuscript.

I was so proud. I'd done it. I sent out my seventy-five thousand word masterpiece to a few friends who liked to read, and whom I hoped would give me some constructive criticism so that I could start querying agents. I was sure it was ready. Instead, I received some very polite, "It's good . . . but . . ." responses. And this was from family and friends. In other words, it was crap.

Facing the hard truth that your work isn't ready, that your baby has flaws, can be devastating. You might be heartbroken and tempted to give up. You hear the word "this needs work" and think you're a terrible writer, that you'll never be any good.

You're wrong. Don't listen to those self-defeating thoughts. Instead, use the criticism to motivate your next steps. When you receive criticism, you can approach it two ways: revise, or start something new. Both have merit.

That first manuscript was a mess. I'd already spent four years working on it, and I couldn't face additional years of edits. Despite the pain of realizing my hard work hadn't amounted to anything anyone would want to read, never mind pay money for, I don't regret a single year or a single word. It was a learning experience and a valuable one. I learned *how* to write a novel, and I proved I could do it. I also discovered the areas of craft in which I needed to improve.

When I went back to the computer again a few months later, I decided I was going to do it right. I spent three months developing the characters and the world they would inhabit. Then spent another year and a half writing the first draft.

After that, it was back to the pits of despair as I sought new feedback from people who actually knew something about the craft of writing. I found my critique partner (see Chapter One), and together we worked chapter by chapter through the novel for another nine months. With each meeting, I faced the pain of criticism, the abject horror of exposing my work to another's eyes. I both eagerly anticipated and feared her comments, but I knew they were necessary to produce a book I could *truly* be proud of.

Finally, I had something that might be publishable. I submitted the first fifteen pages for an advanced reader submission at a local writers' conference. The feedback was extremely positive. I'd taken the time and the necessary steps to build a product a reader would willingly, happily, pay money for.

My first book timeline:

- More than eight years creative writing
- More than two and a half years creating a publishable novel
- Nearly five months from finished, self-edited draft to book launch

All this is to say be proud of your accomplishment. You wrote a book. That's fantastic! But if you're going to take the independent path to publication, you have to put on your business hat and look at the book as a product. Take your time and do it right. Strive for excellence. Ask for criticism from beta readers. Hire editors to make your book better, before you ask readers to spend money on your words. You never get a second chance to make a first impression; so don't leave a bitter taste in readers' mouths.

A Note on Speed to Market

If you're an avid follower of other independent writers, you've probably heard stories of authors who write and publish a full-length novel every year, twice a year, every month . . . even a trilogy in eight weeks.

I'm going to let you in on a little secret: most of those authors have been writing and publishing for a long time. Many of them write as their full-time career. Don't compare yourself to them. It might be a goal to strive for, but don't let it push you to produce less than your best work.

From a marketing perspective, the faster you publish the more money you're going to make. It's true, if only because with each new book, you have a new product for sale. Add on the compounding effect of momentum, and publishing fast can have great benefits. But if you have a full-time job and family responsibilities, you're probably not going to be able to write that quickly and still produce a quality book.

In my opinion, quality trumps quantity. Reputation matters. If you want to build an audience of raving fans, you have to first focus on the craft. However, as you get better and publish more, your speed will improve. I cut my production time in half for my second book, and that was with a newborn and a preschooler at home. I cut it in half again for my third book. But quality always comes first.

Chapter 4

Nice Guys Finish First

The publishing industry is pretty small. When you divide it by genre, it's even smaller. This means you're going to run into the same authors, editors, agents, booksellers, and other professionals again and again. It pays to be nice. Whether you receive a rejection, unkind critique, or praise, the best practice is to say thank you. Thank you for your time. Thank you for your advice. Thank you for the compliment.

When you've found your publishing dream team, it's even more important to be nice. You want to make the most of that experience you've fought so long and hard for. You want to publish a wonderful first book and many more with these people. Here are some common sense pointers on being a great team player.

Traditional Publishing

Your agent, if you have one, will often work as a developmental editor to help ready your book to sell to a publisher. This is a team relationship. You both have something to gain financially from the finished quality. Remember they're the pro here. Generally it's best to take their advice.

Once the book has been sold to a publisher, whether it's a boutique press or one of the big guys, you're now working with editors, cover designers, and marketing people whose main priority is to please the publisher. The publisher pays their salary. However, everybody's goal is to create a product that will sell, and they often know better how to do that than you do. When your stories become as popular as Stephen King's you can throw your weight around, but don't be a prima donna until you've earned it (if at all).

You will be assigned an editor to work with. Generally, you aren't given a choice about whom that person is. This is another reason to vet the publisher well BEFORE you sign with them. If they're known for assigning rookie editors to new authors to save money, are you sure that's the place you want for your work? At the end of this chapter, we've included some tips for working with editors regardless of your publishing path.

Independent Publishing

The relationship between the independent publisher and their team is a bit different than it is for a traditionally published author. You're footing the bill, so *you* are the client. You're also the boss.

You must be sure you're getting what you need. Politely request changes and edits, with the understanding that often the service provider knows more than you do. He or she can produce a better project if you have an open mind and a hands-off attitude.

When I was working with a cover designer on the second book in my series, I wasn't totally thrilled with the model's pose. On the first book's cover there was a sense of action, of movement, but on the new one, it seemed static and still. I politely requested that we look for a different pose.

The designer responded with a link to the photo series available to us. It quickly became clear there wasn't a better option. The photographer who had taken the photos had done about a hundred-fifty poses with the model we'd chosen in the outfit we'd chosen. Only about five or six would work for me. The fact was, the designer had chosen the best possible pose for the second cover.

Demanding impossible changes will result in subpar results. Step back and try to be objective. Even if something doesn't match the image you have in your head, it might be good. Possibly better. In my case, the designer—who'd created hundreds of covers—knew better than I did what would work for my book. Go figure.

A Note on Working with Editors for All Paths to Publication

Editors can be your best friends or your worst enemies; it all depends on how you approach the relationship. Remember, their job is to make your book better. So here are a few tips on making things work to your benefit.

- When you receive feedback from an editor, thank them, read it, put it aside for at least twenty-four hours. Have a little cry if you need to, remind yourself their goal is to improve your book. Don't go back to the manuscript until you've put enough distance between yourself and the criticism to be able to look at it objectively.

- You don't have to take every change as gospel. However, the editor has been hired to give you feedback. A good one has more experience in your genre than you do. Their perspective should be taken seriously.
- In a traditional publishing contract there is generally language about the extent to which editorial changes are mandatory. If changes are too extreme, and you feel your work is being hijacked, you can cancel the contract, but there will be consequences.
- At its best, the author/editor relationship is like a good marriage. There's give and take, an exchange of ideas, communication. Strive to develop that through humility, respect and an open mind.
- If you have a traditional deal and it's impossible to work with the editor you've been assigned, talk to your publisher about making a change for the next book. If you're an indie author, fire them!

SECTION 2

GRIT

"You must pay for everything in this world, one way and another. There is nothing free except the grace of God."

—Mattie Ross, True Grit, 2010

There is an interesting TEDTalk by psychologist Angela Lee Duckworth. Ms. Duckworth and her team studied achievement. Their goal was to isolate predictors of success in all kinds of circumstances. They researched students, business professionals, athletes, people in many walks of life and varieties of endeavors. They found the individuals most likely to succeed all had one quality in common—grit. Ms. Duckworth defines grit as a combination of passion and persistence.

This is something every writer needs in abundance. I don't think it's possible to imagine a piece of work, push past self-doubt to get it written, face the surgery of editing, the labor pains of the publishing process and the arrows of public scrutiny without grit. When a cashier job at Costco seems both less difficult and more lucrative, what else will keep us at the keyboard?

At this point in the book, we'd like to hit the pause button on all the busyness of the publishing process and talk about you, your mindset, your home office, and your organizational skills.

There are three kinds of writers: dreamers, doodlers, and authors. The dreamers won't face reality. Their aim is overnight success, and it often shows in both the quality of their work and their longevity. The doodlers have so little self-esteem or courage their stories never see the light of day.

And then there are authors.

Authors understand there is a road ahead of them and it won't be easy. They know they are going to occasionally lose their way, get mired in the mud, and run out of gas. They plan, they sweat, they swear, but they go the distance. They have grit.

The question then is, how do we get grittier? In the first section of this book, you researched and evaluated possible publishing team members and began the connection process. In this section, you'll be evaluating yourself. The publishing process is hard on many fronts. It's hard practically, and it's hard emotionally. The only way your manuscript will make it from your computer into a published product you're proud of is if you employ GRIT.

G - Goal Setting

R - Revise your calendar

I - Imagine the happy ending

T - Tenacity

Chapter 5

Set SMART Goals

Too often when writers dream of publishing, that's all they do—dream. They either don't set goals, or their goals are, forgive me, kind of dumb. They don't do the hard work of analyzing the process and creating a realistic, attainable action plan.

Businesses without business plans generally fail. You may not want to hear it, but these days successful authors embrace the entrepreneurial aspect of their career. Don't think because your goal is to find an agent, you are exempt. You'll be more likely to find and keep an agent if you have this mindset. Whatever path to publication you've chosen to follow, you need SMART goals to keep you on track.

Goals Must Be:

Specific • **M**easurable • **A**ttainable • **R**ealistic • **T**ime-bound

Be Specific:

Unless your goals are specific, how can you plan appropriately? How do you know when you've accomplished what you need to accomplish? Hopefully this will be an easy question for you to answer after working through the material in the ReCON section of the book, but write it down anyway. Goals that are written are forty-two percent more likely to be achieved than unwritten goals according to a study done by Dr. Gail Matthews, a psychology professor at the Dominican University in California.

Examples of Specific Goals Would Be:

- I want to publish my own book.
- I want to find a boutique publisher to publish my finished novel.
- I want to sign with a literary agent and lean on their expertise to sell my finished novel.

Make the Goals Measurable:

Now that you've written down the basic goal, let's make sure it's measurable. Measurable goals have distinct parameters. For instance, in the world of fitness your specific goal might be to run a race. To make that goal measurable you'd say, I want to run a 5K. Now you know how to train.

- I want to publish my own book utilizing industry professionals for editing, graphics and formatting in both digital and print on demand.
- I want to find a boutique publisher who will create digital versions of my book and will also do print runs and sell my books to bookstores.

- I want to sign with a literary agent who has a good track record selling stories in the genre I write to reputable publishing houses.

Make the Goals Attainable:

Sometimes writers don't set publishing goals because they feel they have so little control over the process, especially those seeking outside representation. It's important to make sure your goal is attainable.

Signing a contract with an agent or a publishing house, or even finding the perfect independent publishing dream team, is a lot like finding a spouse. There's uncertainty and faith involved.

In order to make our above goals into things we have control over, we might need to reword them.

- I want to follow five blogs, or podcasts on the topic of independent publishing so that I can publish my own book utilizing industry professionals for editing, graphics, and formatting in both digital and print on demand.
- I want to find and pitch twenty boutique publishers who will create digital versions of my book and will also do print runs and sell my books to bookstores.
- I want to find and pitch twenty literary agents who have a good track record selling stories in the genre I write to reputable publishing houses.

Be Realistic

The Realistic part of your SMART goal is the *quality control* section and can be the most uncomfortable to challenge. Going back to the fitness analogy, if my client was planning to run their first 5K, I would discourage them from setting a time goal. If they'd never run that distance before, they wouldn't know their capabilities. Instead, I'd suggest a training program that included mini-goals of ever-increasing distances to get them ready. The mini-goals would reveal their strengths and weaknesses, so we would know what to work on.

Ask yourself: are you ready to be published? How do you know? Has someone besides your mother read your work and critiqued it well? If you've started pitching, have you only received form letters as rejections?

If so, maybe you should consider creating some preliminary mini-goals that focus on craft.

Realistic mini-goals:

- Find objective critique partners.
- Get a smaller work published in an anthology, magazine, or other commercial publication.
- Take a novel writing course with a teacher who will give you feedback.

Don't be afraid to write and rewrite your goals. The reason New Year's resolutions routinely fail is because they're set once, without much thought. When it becomes obvious they're not going to be met, people feel like failures and give up. But the problem isn't the person, it's the goal. Unrealistic expectations are just that, unrealistic.

Define Your Timeline

The final letter in your SMART goal stands for Time-bound. If you don't set a deadline by which to accomplish your goal, it will probably never happen. Goals are simply dreams with a deadline.

In order to do this without sabotaging yourself, you have to take the entirety of your life into consideration. If you work full time and have a house full of kids you're shuffling from school to soccer to ballet, there's only so much of you to go around. Writing a novel is time consuming. Now add to that working on your craft, researching vendors and publishers, creating a query letter, auditioning editors, starting a website, participating in social media, and . . . you get the picture.

How much time can you carve out of your already busy schedule to do all the things you're going to need to do? What are you willing to give up? Think this through carefully. Now go back through all the sections of SMART and write your new goal with a realistic date. In the next chapter, we'll tackle breaking that big goal into manageable steps and plotting those steps on the calendar.

Chapter 6

Revise Your Calendar

Now that you have a goal in mind, it's time to make it real. Write it down and post it somewhere prominent in your house or at your desk. Then announce it to the world. Share your goals with supportive family and friends, with your writing group, and in your online community.

Why? Because it forces you to accept that you have a dream, and you're working to achieve that dream. But making a goal is not the end of the road. It's just the beginning. If you really want to achieve your dreams, you have to break them down into manageable steps.

Step One: Final Deadline

Start with a target launch date. With a date in mind, you can determine your milestones and intermediate deadlines. Deadlines are the bane of many people's existence, but without them no one accomplishes anything.

If you're pursuing either the traditional agented path, or the traditional boutique press, you're probably starting to wonder if this section is for you. It is. Bear with me.

The launch date does not have to be the date your book is published and available for sale. That's true for independent authors, but traditional authors don't have enough control to make that an attainable or realistic goal. Instead, your launch date may be the date you send a manuscript to an agent, or show it to an editor. This could be at a conference through the advanced submission process. Or, it could be the date you send out your first query. (Your manuscript is polished and ready in case they immediately request a full manuscript, right?)

In the beginning, while you're still writing the first draft, you can keep things a little vague. Something like, "I want to send my first query letter in June" or "I want to publish Book 3 in June." That works . . . until it doesn't. As soon as you start hiring other professionals to work on your project, or register for a conference, you'll need to be more specific. Your deadlines must be reasonable. For the purposes of our example, let's use June 30th as the final deadline for both processes.

Step Two: Milestones and Intermediate Deadlines

I'm going to assume you've already selected the agents, editors, and service providers you want to connect with. If not, go back and read Section One. Once that's done, we can start to build a timeline. There are two main questions to consider when filling out your calendar:

- How much time does each task require?
- Are there dependencies to the order in which they operate?

For example, if you're going to send your manuscript to a developmental editor, how much time does she need to complete her work? And what do you have to do before you can send her the manuscript? If she has a two-week turnaround, and you still have at least two weeks of work before you can send it, then you're at least four-weeks away from launch date. Add in an estimated two weeks (or whatever seems reasonable) for incorporating her suggestions into the next draft, and you're really at least six-weeks away from launch.

There are also tasks that aren't dependent on others' work, like the cover design. If you're an independent author who needs to hire a cover designer, you can do that at any time. As I write this, I have a cover designed and ready for a book I haven't even written yet. The only caveat is that the cover must be finalized before you run a reveal or submit files for publication. Can you see where I'm going with this? Here are few more possible tasks to consider, grouped by publication path:

Traditional Publishing

- Manuscript preparation
- Beta reader critiques
- Read and review programs
- Professional editing
- Writing the book synopsis
- Conferences
- Query letters

Independent Publishing

- Professional editing
- Cover design
- Formatting

- Writing descriptions
- Filing the copyright
- Scheduling promotions
- Creating teasers and other promotional imagery
- Uploading to distributors: Amazon, Createspace, Smashwords, etc.

Obviously, this isn't an exhaustive list. But hopefully it has you thinking about the tasks you need to accomplish to reach your goals.

Step Three: Get Out Your Calendar

At this point, we've decided on our target date (June 30) and you know at least some of the tasks that need to be completed, how long they'll take, and their order of operation. Now it's time to create your timeline. You can use a calendar, or even a word file. Let's walk through the process together, using the independent publishing model.

Keep in mind, the *process* for creating a timeline is the same for traditional publishing, but the *tasks* are different. For example, traditionally published authors won't have control over the launch date or be responsible for formatting. But they will have deadlines for edits and other tasks that can be plotted out on a calendar.

Now, let's get started.

First: what needs to happen immediately before our launch date?

- Advanced reviewers need to receive an Advanced Reader Copy (ARC), with enough time to read and prepare a review, preferably one month: May 31st.

- Which means the manuscript must be formatted and ready by May 30th.
- Prior to that, we need to incorporate the copy editor's comments. This can take up to a week, so they need to be done by May 23rd at the latest.
- The copy editor needs a month for her work, so they'll start on April 23rd.

Now let's add in some of the marketing tasks. I like to run a cover reveal on as many book blogs as I can find. The cover reveal needs to happen at least a couple weeks before the book launch.

Cover reveal task list:

- Cover reveal: June 15th
- The final cover and all related material (book description, author bio, etc.) need to be submitted to the book bloggers who want to participate at least a few days prior to the reveal so they can set up their posts: June 12th
- But we need to get them signed up first! This takes some time, so starting sooner rather than later is a good idea. How about one month: May 12th.

Again, this is not a comprehensive project plan. Each book launch or major deadline will have at least a few unique elements. This is an example of the process you should go through to plot your larger, macro goals. Writing them down in a timeline or calendar will keep you accountable and move your writing goals forward.

Check your calendar every day, or at least once a week. Look at the day, and the month as a whole, so nothing creeps up on you. Revise the schedule as needed. Add new deadlines and milestones when appropriate. Be flexible, but don't give yourself excuses for not getting your work done. If you truly want to be a published author, you have to get your butt in your chair, your fingers on your keyboard, and focus.

Chapter 7

Imagine the Finish Line

There's a statement that's touted in life coach and business guru circles: if you can imagine yourself doing something, you can achieve it. But is it true?

An exercise psychologist from the Cleveland Clinic Foundation in Ohio, Guang Yue, conducted an interesting experiment. He used two control groups, one went to the gym and worked out with weights, the other performed the same workout in their imaginations. Unsurprisingly, the group that actually went to the gym achieved a 30% increase in muscle mass.

What was a shocker though, was the group who worked through the routine in their heads increased strength by 13.5% without ever picking up a dumbbell. Before you close the computer, put your feet up and daydream your way through an exercise routine, let's think this through. Why does this work?

Vivid mental images fire neurons in the brain. Those signals travel down the spinal column and enervate the muscles just like real experiences do. In fact, many scientists believe your brain can't tell the difference between the two.

Athletes and coaches have utilized this technique for decades. I incorporated many meditations in my book *The Wine and Chocolate Workout* to help people get up off the couch and start a fitness routine. Then why has visualization gotten such bad press recently?

Another study done in New York University's Motivation Lab found that daydreams decreased motivation. People who indulged in fantasies about the cute guy asking them out, or a test paper with a big "A" at the top were less likely to achieve their dreams. Why does visualization work for athletes and not for NYU's student body?

The answer to that question takes us back to G in our GRIT challenge—goal setting. It seems my grandmother was correct when she said, "Wish in one hand, spit in the other, and see which gets full first."

To quote another wise dearly departed, Aristotle, "First, have a definite, clear, practical ideal; a goal, an objective. Second, have the necessary means to achieve your ends: wisdom, money, materials, and methods. Third, adjust all your means to that end."

Visualization isn't a magic formula as some would have you believe. It's one ingredient, one tool, to help you achieve your goals. When it comes to creativity and accomplishment, we're often our own worst enemy. What is writer's block if it isn't fear of failure? Why can we manage to find the time to check Facebook forty-five times a day but have no time to finish our query letter? Why does one bad review wipe out the impact of ten positive ones?

I believe premeditated, structured visualization turns your subconscious from enemy to ally. Stephen King calls his muse "the boys in the basement." I like that analogy. Imagine you have a gang sitting at their typewriters chomping cigars ready to tap out your dictation. What's the story you're telling them to write?

Visualization triggers your brain to work toward a goal. When you decide you're going to buy a car, you start noticing the make and model you're thinking about purchasing. All of sudden it's everywhere. Of course, it was there all the time, but your brain was busy filtering it out. You hadn't told "the boys" it was important, and there are only so many things you can focus on at a time.

I challenge you to take charge of your subconscious and begin to bend your mind toward your goal. You're a writer. Write a short scene with yourself as the main character. Imagine yourself achieving your SMART goal. Where are you? What are you wearing? What do you see, smell, feel, hear? Use your senses. I suggest you keep this handy and visit it every day. Read it out loud whenever possible.

CHAPTER 8

TENACITY

A tenacious person is determined—unwilling to give up their dreams. A tenacious person is steadfast. They grab a hold of something and never let go. Yet, tenacity as a concept for a creative endeavor can be hard to pin down. Sure, we all want to be writers. We all want to be successful. I *say* I'm determined to make a full-time income from my fiction, but when the road to financial success looks like a cross-country trek it's easy to make a pit stop and get lost along the way.

How do we keep going in the face of rejection? How do we get back on track, when life intrudes? Moreover, how do we stay focused on the finish line when it looks like a mirage in the distance?

Have you ever heard of the Seinfeld Strategy? There's a story about a young comedian (Brad Isaac) who slipped backstage after a show one day and asked Jerry Seinfeld (arguably the most successful comedian on the face of the planet) if he had any advice. Here's what Brad had to say about the encounter:

> *"He told me to get a big wall calendar that has a whole year on one page and hang it on a prominent wall. The next step was to get a big red magic marker.*
>
> *He said for each day that I do my task of writing, I get to put a big red X over that day. 'After a few days you'll have a chain. Just keep at it and the chain will grow longer every day. You'll like seeing that chain, especially when you get a few weeks under your belt. Your only job is to not break the chain.'"* [1]

Don't break the chain. That's it. Consistency in a nutshell. But how do we do it? How do we build the habits needed to keep that chain going?

There's an article that was posted to creativity website 99U titled "5 Scientific Ways to Build Habits That Stick: Eliminate "ah-screw-its" and other ways to make that new habit last for the long haul."[2]

In their estimation, the number one method to make and keep a habit was to create "micro quotas" and "macro goals." What does that mean?

If you've been reading this book chronologically, then you should have already identified your macro goals. You've chosen your preferred path to publication, and you've created a basic project plan or timeline that will help get you there. Micro quotas are simply the smallest daily tasks that can be accomplished to move you forward.

To make this example simple, let's talk about the universal goal for any writer: the completion of a first draft. You have your deadline, right? That day when the first draft needs to be finished so you can send it off to your editor or beta readers or critique group? Good. How many words per day do you need to write to finish your draft by that day? That could be your micro quota. Or you might need to think even smaller.

I'm not a fast writer. At least, not yet. But I want to get faster, so I challenged myself with a short (for me) deadline. To reach my eighty thousand word estimated manuscript length, I needed to write about fifteen hundred words per working day.

Fifteen hundred words was difficult for me. A significant challenge. Trying to keep that up over multiple, consecutive days seemed like a monumental task. If I missed a day, I became demotivated. Or, I would try to reassure myself that I could "make it up tomorrow," except that meant I needed three thousand words the next day. I felt totally overwhelmed. I ended up stressed out, filled with negative thoughts and emotions. I had to make a change or I would not only miss my self-imposed deadline, I might quit writing the book altogether. Not acceptable.

I changed my mindset. Instead of demanding huge goals of myself each and every day—goals that might be theoretically feasible, but extremely challenging to maintain long-term—I decided on an impossible-not-to-achieve micro goal: work on my manuscript every day.

I might write one sentence, or five thousand words. I might spend ten minutes at my desk, or two hours. But I worked on the manuscript *every single day*.

What kind of progress can be achieved with such low standards? You'd be amazed. Just setting the habit of sitting down to work every day increased my productivity. In the beginning there were plenty of days that I was happy to get a hundred words on the page. Fifty. But within a week or two, my averages were improving. Soon it was easy to sit down and write. My brain and my fingers knew what was expected of them. Eventually, I was regularly exceeding my original fifteen-hundred word goal.

Do I miss some days? Of course. I'm not perfect. But when I do, I get up and keep going the next day. Because all I need to do is write *something*. And with my calendar in hand, checking off those days and meeting those deadlines is easy.

Start with the simplest micro quota and macro goal: work on your manuscript every day for five days in a row. Use that red pen to cross out the days on your calendar. Don't break the chain. Then celebrate. You're starting a new habit and becoming a gritty writer.

SECTION 3

NoEGO

"I don't care if a reader hates one of my stories, just as long as he finishes the book."

—Roald Dahl, Writer's Digest

You've chosen your publishing path, researched and begun the process of finding industry professionals, established your long-term goals, and scheduled your micro-goals. What's left to do? Plenty.

Imagine you've decided to start a vegetable garden. The ReCON section of this book could be compared to the planning stages of this endeavor. You've poured over the seed catalogues, determined which plants are best for your climate, learned the growth patterns, and maybe even ordered a package of seeds, or a plant or two.

In the GRIT stages of gardening, you plotted the perimeter of the space, turned the soil, fertilized, planted your seeds, and started watering. Now it's time to get ready for a harvest.

We have a peach tree. On a good year we get hundreds of peaches. That's something I have to prepare for. If I don't, the fruit rots on the ground and makes a mess in my backyard. I need a system, or systems, to use the produce. I give some away. I pull out my peach recipes. I freeze some, and I don't plan any long trips during harvest.

You need systems in place to reap the fruit of your labors. There's nothing sadder than a well-written, well-produced book languishing on Amazon—unless it's an author who gets a book contract, but never gets another because they didn't deliver what they'd promised.

In this section, we'll be laying the foundation of your author career: uncovering the platform options that are right for you, evaluating your potential audience, building systems for growth, and deciding on your next project.

No - When to say it

E - Evaluate your audience

G - Grow your reach

O - Onward, seeing past book one

CHAPTER 9

NO: WHEN TO SAY IT

Many writers want to wait until their first book is published before they start thinking about their audience and how best to reach them. They mistakenly focus on craft and execution, to the exclusion of readers and fans. It doesn't matter which path to publication you choose to pursue, you must have an author platform. Problem is, there are so many options it's easy to become overwhelmed.

How are you supposed to know what's necessary, and what's not? There are already too many demands on our time. Not only do you have to write your minimum word count, but now you're being told you also have to start blogging, networking, participating in social media, and making publicity appearances. You have to build an author platform. What does that even mean?

An Author Platform

According to publishing expert Jane Friedman, an author platform is "an ability to sell books because of who you are or who you can reach."[2] It is being visible to readers, and engaging with your target audience (we'll learn more about your target reader in Chapter Ten). But it's not just about the numbers.

Developing an author platform is essential for building your author career, but it can be expensive in both time and resources. How many hours do you spend whiling away time on social media, writing blog posts instead of novels, or fiddling with the settings on your website? Or maybe you've spent hundreds of dollars on a blog tour or publicity campaign, with no proof of a return on your investment.

Publicity—or public attention—always costs you something, even when it's free. So how do you decide which opportunities to jump on, and which ones to say no to? Some of that will become more clear when you evaluate your audience in the next chapter. For now, we're going to look at the most common options for building your author platform, with the benefits and drawbacks of each. We'll help you weed out the unnecessary, say yes to the things that will grow your fanbase, and say no to those that waste your time or money.

The Website

The website is the one thing that is truly non-negotiable. Every author needs one, if only so that you have a place to showcase your books all in one place. We'll get into the details of setting up a basic website in Chapter Eleven, but you should think about how you want to use your website to build your author platform. There are a lot of options.

Domain Name

Your first step is to decide on a domain name. I highly recommend you own your domain, but before you go out and buy something that will be a waste of money in the long-term, think through the kind of website you want to have. For example, fiction authors should probably stick with their author name, or their penname. This gives a single location for your readers to visit, but at the same time provides the flexibility to expand your site as you publish more books. You can always have a page for each book, or if you write multiple series, a page for each series.

Nonfiction writers may choose a different method to select their domain name—their name, a version of their book title, or perhaps something related to their subject matter. Keep in mind, the website is a way to collectively brand your books under a common name or theme.

Although a growing number of people will simply Google your name instead of typing in the URL, having a domain that is your name or your brand helps ensure that you come up first in the search results, or at least on the first page. That said, I strongly discourage fiction writers from getting a domain for a single book or series. If you want to have a career as an author, you're going to write more books, and the more books you have, the more complicated it would be to manage separate websites for each title or series.

Think carefully about your domain name. If your first choice isn't available (more on that in Chapter Eleven), try a variation. Make it as easy as possible for your readers to find you, remember you, and tell others about your site.

Website Content

Once you have your domain selected, it's time to think about the content you want on the site. An 'About' page is a must, with an author biography and typically a nice-looking picture of you. You might also want a page for each of your books, or for each series if you have a large backlist. At a minimum, book pages should have the cover image, description, and maybe a free sample or a selection of your best reviews. Start to write and gather the bits and pieces of information you want to share, so it's ready to go when you start building your site.

Should You Blog?

Now, what about a blog? There are people who argue that every author should have a blog on their personal website. For nonfiction authors, this is very good advice. You can write about your topic, share articles and insights into your research, develop a reputation as an expert in your field, and generally start to draw in a group of people interested in your subject matter. In some cases, the blog posts themselves can be modified and turned into a book—recipes, parenting, and writing craft authors have all done this successfully. And you can do all of this before your book is available for sale, giving your book launch a definite boost from an audience already prepped and willing to hit that buy button as soon as it's available for sale.

The answer isn't as clear-cut for fiction writers. Some authors have used blogs to great success. Andy Weir, author of mega bestseller *The Martian*, is a perfect example. He started writing sci-fi in his twenties and published his work to his own website. *The Martian* began as a serialized novel on his blog. He also posted about his research and the steps he was taking to ensure accuracy for the novel. Eventually, his readers wanted the story compiled into a single manuscript, so he self-published the book on Amazon. When sales soared, he was approached by an agent, who sold print rights to Crown Publishing Group, and on to the movie studios. In other words, he built his audience long before he brought in a book deal.

That doesn't necessarily mean you should try to copy Andy Weir's success. Quite frankly, he's an outlier. But if you're comfortable posting your work in serialized form for free, it's a model to consider.

On the other hand, some fiction writers don't find blogging helpful, myself included. In fact, I chose to quit my fiction blog altogether. I wasn't comfortable posting an unedited serial, because my books require a lot of plot editing after the entire first draft is written. So when I started blogging, I tried to write about my research, world building, and process. I would stress over what to post next, struggling to find relevant content that would draw in new readers. I didn't enjoy the process at all.

In the end, I felt my time and energy would be much better spent writing my novel, rather than writing *about* my novel. The blog was taking too much time away from my work in progress, and it wasn't attracting new fans and followers. It was a stressful addition to an already overloaded schedule. Instead, I chose to pare down my reader outreach to a once-a-month newsletter and quick Facebook updates so that I could focus on quality over quantity, and producing my next novel . . . which is what my fans really want, anyway.

Was that the right decision? For me, it was. As a publicity tactic, a personal blog wasn't worth the cost. Don't be afraid to constantly reevaluate where you're spending your resources in order to get the most bang for your proverbial buck.

Blogging and Article Writing for Other Websites

Even if you choose to forego the personal blog, writing for magazines or websites that have a bigger following than you do can be a great way for new authors get their names into the public arena. A short story published in a literary magazine, online or in paper, is not just an audience builder, you might even get paid, and it looks great on your resume.

There are many websites and blogs looking for content that you might be able to provide. Book bloggers want author interviews and guest posts. Writer's websites need how-to articles and advice on craft. Nonfiction authors could target blogs and websites in their topic area, and fiction authors can pursue genre-targeted fan sites.

Often, the compensation provided by other blogs and websites is a link back to your personal website or your published works. It's free publicity and can be a great way to build your credibility. But writing quality articles takes time, time that could be spent working on your next book. How do you decide if it's really worthwhile?

By this point, you must have realized a calendar is an essential weapon in the professional writer's arsenal. I firmly believe every writer should have some kind of calendar, organizer, or planner. It doesn't matter if it's digital or paper, if you have a dedicated app on your phone or a six-inch binder, so long as it has space to write down dates and events. If you don't have one, go get one.

Now take a look at your schedule. If you have deadlines looming, it's probably not a good choice to add more work. However, even if there aren't any immediate conflicts on your calendar, you're a working writer. Your manuscript should take precedence over any other writing. So the next question becomes, what are the benefits of writing for the site, and what is the true cost?

A byline and link to your books can increase your visibility in the market and boost your ranking on Google. You might even sell a few books if you're already published, especially if the website has a large, targeted audience. Plus, there are the added benefits of establishing yourself as an expert or giving back to the community. The perks may make it worth your time.

On the other hand, there are no guarantees that you'll see any benefits from the post. Even if you do, you might not be able to quantify them. Larger, more prominent blogs will have bigger bonuses, but you'll also have to spend more time producing a high-quality article that they'll be interested in publishing.

Yes, or no? In the end, there's no clear answer. Each situation will be different, each project requiring its own analysis. But never be afraid to say no, if you need to.

Social Media

Much like blogging, there are those who say every author should be active on Facebook, or Twitter, or Instagram, or Pinterest, or Tumblr, or . . . you name it. The fact is, you could tweet and post twenty-four hours a day and not cover all the available social media sites. What works for one author, might not work for you. Moreover, each social media site attracts a different kind of user.

We talk more about the nitty-gritty of social media in Chapter Eleven, but when you're thinking about joining a new platform, there are a few major points to consider:

- Do you enjoy it? If not, it's probably not going to work for you, and you should probably say no.
- Is your target audience active on the platform? (We'll talk about this more in Chapters Ten and Eleven.) If yes, you might want to find a way to like it even if you don't right now.
- Is there an active writing community on the platform? Sometimes it's not about how many books you can sell today, but the connections you make which can potentially lead to more sales down the road.
- How will you make connections? Always remember, social media is just that—*social.* Whatever you choose to do, don't spam the interwebs with "buy my book" posts. Instead, use the networks to engage with fans and colleagues as a real, live person.
- How much time do you really have to spend? Social media can be a significant time sink. The more platforms you engage on, the more time you'll be spending *not* working on your manuscript. You have to say no to something.

Networking

Getting out and about is a great way to meet other writers, learn about industry opportunities, and maybe even engage with readers with the possibility of selling books. Should you take the time to attend a writing event, like a conference or workshop? When you say yes, you have to say no to something else.

Every month, there's a local author event at a coffee shop near me. A friend of mine hosts the evening, three authors are invited to read from their books, and then the crowd discusses the work. It's a lot of fun, and a great way to associate yourself with the literary community.

One particular month, I desperately wanted to go hear a friend read. I love his book, and I knew he would be great behind the mic. Also, our genres are similar. His fans are potentially my future fans. It would have been a good place to show my face. Unfortunately, I was also working on the edits of my latest manuscript, and yes, I had a deadline looming. I knew I couldn't afford to lose a night's work so as much as it pained me, I had to say no.

However, there are a few events and conferences that I make sure to attend, planning for them well in advance and setting aside time on my calendar. The rest of my schedule—including deadlines and publication dates—is built around these networking activities. Why? Because it's at these events that I have made lasting connections with other writers and readers. In fact, I met Greta at a conference, and look where we are today!

Paid Publicity

Big league publicists set up book signing tours, radio shows, TV interviews, and online tours, but they're often very expensive to hire. The return on investment is also much harder to calculate than, say, a paid product ad. When you run an Amazon ad for your new book, you can watch what happens to sales, subtract the cost of the ad, and, voila! You now have a pretty good idea if it was worth the investment.

The value of public appearances is more difficult to calculate. If you visit three bookstores and sell thirty books, but the cost of booking that tour was a grand, it looks like a loss. However, the people who attended may feel a deeper connection and loyalty to you because they met you in person. If a few of them turn into super-fans—people who buy everything you write and tell everyone they know about you—maybe it was worth the cost.

There are also some less expensive options, including online publicists who will set up blog tours, review teams, Facebook launch parties, and social media blasts. These individuals or companies may only charge a few hundred dollars for their services, often in an a la carte menu from which you can choose. However, be warned—if the publicist isn't connected to your genre, you might not get much activity.

Final Thought

At this point, you should have some ideas for how you might want to build your author platform. Keep an open mind, but critically consider each option. Look at your finances, your calendar, the pros and cons of each opportunity, then ask yourself these simple questions: will this activity advance my writing career? Will this project, or conference, or social media platform, or event bring me closer to becoming the writer that I want to be? If the answer is no, your response is obvious. Chuck it. If it's yes, or maybe, you still have some strategizing to do. In the next two chapters, we'll give you more tools to help you decide which of the myriad of possible building blocks you should choose for your author brand.

Chapter 10

Evaluate Your Audience

In order to evaluate our audience, we need to harken back to our initial motivation for writing our book and be honest with ourselves. It probably had something to do with the story we wanted to tell, or the message we wanted to put out into the world. Unless you're a subject-matter expert writing non-fiction, you probably didn't consider your target market. Unfortunately, many writers are caught in a terrible love triangle between their protagonist and their audience.

I took the advice to "write what you know" a bit too literally in the beginning. In my first fiction attempts, my protagonist did nothing but walk her dog around her Southern California neighborhood and fret about what she was going to do with her life. Boring.

Even the parts of the story I intended to be exciting didn't put her at risk. I didn't want her life to be any more uncomfortable than it already was. I was in love with my protagonist. She was me—my offspring, and the fruit of my imagination.

Likewise, nonfiction writers can become enamored with their personal experience, opinions, and attitudes. It's their book, after all. They want to say what they want to say, the way they want to say it.

Slowly but surely, through numerous agent and editor rejections and my own analysis of the books I enjoyed, I learned the error of my ways. If I wanted my books to sell, it couldn't be all about me. It had to be all about the reader. Readers want to be wooed and fascinated. They want thrills and chills. They want to grow and learn.

What would they do if they were kidnapped by a serial killer? If their child were lost? If their business were to go bankrupt, and they had to rebuild from nothing? Don't get me wrong, they don't actually want to experience those things, but they do want to challenge problems from the safety of their armchairs. It doesn't matter if you're writing fiction, memoir, or a narrative non-fiction; readers want to live vicariously. Even how-to books are often peppered with other people's experiences so readers can imagine themselves going through the process before they actually do.

How to Please Your Reader:

The first step in learning to please your audience is to narrow the field. Your book isn't for everyone. One of the most common misconceptions writers have is thinking they will lose sales if they aim at only one type of person. They're afraid to limit their market.

It's much easier to grow into a large fish in a small pond. If you jump into a large pond before you're big enough, you end up as fish food. Look at bestsellers and you'll see even the big fish define their audience. Nora Roberts' covers don't look like Stephen King's, or Dan Brown's. Their marketing copy reads entirely different. That's because they're each aiming at a different reader.

There is some trial and error in the quest for your ideal reader, but there are also practical steps you can take. One is to look at the authors who are selling well in your genre. Not just your broad genre, but the subgenres as well. Readers of sweet western romance don't like erotica even though they're both romance. Drill down. Look at what those authors are doing, what they're saying, how their marketing copy reads, what their websites look like. Go back to the genre defining exercise in Chapter One and repeat the process, this time with a marketing mindset.

Once you understand the reader you're aiming at, what attracts them, the language they prefer, the themes they enjoy, you can use that information to polish and publish your book, set up your website, and write your marketing copy.

The Invisible Reader

Another great way to understand your audience is to write directly to an invisible reader. Somewhere in the process of revising *A Margin of Lust* with my editor, I began tweaking dialog and changing story lines with her face (and her red pen) in my mind. I began to understand what she liked, and what she didn't. I wanted to please. All of a sudden my reader had a name. It changed everything

When I began book two in my series, I understood the importance of writing for a reader. This time, instead of thinking about my editor, I used my imagination to create a new character, Rachel Reader. I saw her in my mind lounging in her backyard with a glass of wine, or cuddled by the fireplace with a cup of tea. Oh, and my book.

And guess what? She couldn't put it down. I tweaked dialog and changed story lines to keep her riveted. I put my protagonist through the wringer, but threaded in moments of humor and warmth in the hopes Rachel would keep coming back for more.

The dog didn't die in act two, he just got very sick—Rachel wouldn't like a dead dog. But someone stalked the protagonist through a dark parking lot—got to keep Rachel awake and turning pages.

If you make your reader as real as any of your characters, you can write to please her. When the book is done, you'll intuitively know what kind of cover she'd prefer, what types of author events she'd be tempted to attend.

I realize some of you may be moaning. Why didn't you tell us this in Chapter One when we were just getting started? You may have heard it said that writing is rewriting. I believe it. Especially for first books.

If you've managed to get a book contract between Chapters One and Chapters Ten, or if you've decided to independently publish and you've hired an editor, you're probably being led through the process of making your book a more salable product. Writing to an audience isn't productive on the first draft of your first book. But now that you've been around the block a few times, you're ready for the challenge. Once you understand your audience, you can begin to grow it.

Chapter 11

Grow Your Reach

You have a book. You want to be a successful author, which means you need to sell your book to people other than your family and friends. Your mom can only buy so many copies, after all.

In Chapter Nine, we talked about some of the options for building your author platform. Hopefully, that gave you some idea of the types of publicity and marketing activities that you're interested in. Then, in Chapter Ten, we talked about your audience. Who is your Rachel Reader? Now, let's build our platform and go find her.

Author Website:

We've established that an author website is an absolute must. Whether or not you choose to include a blog, whatever domain name you've chosen, you now need to build the hub for your author brand. It doesn't have to be complicated, and you don't have to spend hundreds or thousands of dollars hiring a web developer. You can do everything on your own in just a few simple steps.

1. Own Your Own Domain.

Remember, this should be your author name or an easy (for the reader) to remember URL that relates to your books and your personal brand. If your name isn't available, add "author" or "writes" or something similar until you find an easy URL that is.

There are several domain registries where you can buy your domain. GoDaddy.com and Hover.com are both decent options to search for and purchase your chosen domain, but you can often also purchase your name through your website builder. When you do the search, the registry will tell you if your domain name is available, how much it costs to purchase, and some alternatives that might be less expensive.

Tips:

- Try as hard as you can to get a .com domain. These are the easiest for readers to remember *by far.*
- Don't buy vanity domains, like .fun or .irish. Keep it simple. If you absolutely can't find a .com that you like, choose something that makes sense and is memorable.
- Avoid dashes. For example, if your name is Jane Doe, but www.janedoe.com isn't available, try to avoid www.jane-doe.com. Why? Say it out loud! It's a bit of a tongue-twister, and therefore harder to remember. Instead, try out www.janedoeauthor.com or www.janedoewrites.com. Be creative!
- Remember, while a growing number of people don't actively type the domain into their browser (they search

on Google instead) your domain will still be written on everything from business cards to the back of your book.

2. Site Building Company

At the time of this writing, there are several website builders you can choose from, though WordPress, Squarespace, Wix, and Weebly are perhaps the best known. I tend to think WordPress is the PC of the hosting sites: very powerful, many options and add-ons, but generally more complicated than the other sites. The others are like Macs: easy to use straight out of the box, but not as customizable. Take a look at all of them. You can even sign up for a free account and test them out for awhile to see which you like best. But ultimately, pick one.

Once you've signed up, connect your domain name, or purchase it through the hosting company. There should be clear instructions on how to do this, but we've included a few websites with instructions in the resources page in Appendix 2 on page 127.

3. Select a Theme

Now it's just a matter of choosing a template and setting up a few basic pages. It doesn't have to be fancy, and you can always change your mind later. You should have a page for your book(s), an author bio, and a blog, if you've chosen to go that route. The theme should be clean and easy to read, and it should fit with your author branding.

Blog

As mentioned in Chapter Nine, blogging can be an extremely valuable tool for building an audience when it's used correctly. If you've decided to incorporate blogging into your author platform, and have built a page on your website for the blog, there are a few dos and don'ts you should be aware of.

- DO: Keep a consistent schedule. Keep in mind—especially in the beginning—the more frequently you post, the faster you'll build content. That said, don't burn yourself out or focus on the blog to the detriment of your book. Consistency is key. Set and then meet reader expectations. If you're going to post once a week, do it, and try to keep it on the same day. If you're going to post once a month, same thing. Every day? More power to you!
- DON'T: Blog about writing unless you want to build an audience of writers. This is a mistake many fiction authors make. It's easy to come up with posts about the craft of writing, or the writing process. The writing community is very active so those posts are likely to get a lot of shares. Unfortunately, not all writers will be readers of your genre (unless you're writing nonfiction for writers) so that audience might not carry over to your fiction very well.
- DO: Always consider Rachel Reader. What does she want to know? What are her passions? Do you share them? Write about those things. These posts will reach the hearts and minds of your target audience.
- DON'T: Forget to write your book. Sometimes a blog can lead to a book. Sometimes it's just a distraction from your true goal—a completed and published manuscript.

- DO: Make sure to share your blog posts on social media. If you don't get the word out, no one else will do it for you. In addition to Facebook and Twitter, consider reader forums, fan sites, and other places where Rachel Readers congregate.

Newsletter or Mailing List

Once you've built your website, the next step is to begin gathering your fans. The best way to do this is with a mailing list. In fact, the number one asset an author has, outside of his or her books, is the newsletter mailing list. This is made up of people who have entrusted you with their email address, because they enjoy your work and want to know more. With a mailing list, you don't have to worry about whether or not Amazon will promote your book, or if Facebook will show your post to the people who like your page. In both of those cases, and any other social media you use, the platform controls your connection to your fans. But if you build your own list, you control everything. You own the list. Even if you change platforms, you can take your list with you.

We'll talk more about how to get people to sign up for your list in Section Four, but I want to cover the basics of set up here.

There are several well-respected mailing list service providers to choose from. Perhaps the best known is Mailchimp, but there are at least a dozen others, including MailerLite, Aweber, Emma, and ActiveCampaign. Each of these has some level of free use, usually with a maximum number of subscribers and a few limitations on the features. For the most part, when you're just starting out, any one of them will do. Choose the one you like, and open an account. Set up a form for your fans to subscribe to your list. Spend some time playing around with the features and familiarizing yourself with the layout. Create a test email and send it to yourself to see how it looks.

When it comes to building the content for your newsletter, it's important to once again consider your Rachel Reader. What does she want to hear from you? New release announcements? Probably. Excerpts, giveaways, and other free content? Most likely. Promotions for other authors? Maybe. Buy my book ads? Unlikely.

Just like with blogging, whatever you choose to do, whatever rules you put in place for your newsletter, it's important to set and fulfill reader expectations, maintain a consistent schedule, and engage with your readers. Your reader is first and foremost.

Social Media

I believe every author should be on at least one social media platform. Think about Rachel Reader. Where does she hang out online? That's where you want to be.

Don't go crazy though. You don't need to join every new trendy website or spend hours posting selfies with your dog. (Although, selfies with your dog do tend to get a lot of 'likes'.) The important thing is to find a place where you as an author are comfortable and where you can connect with your readers.

Pick one site at a time and try it out. Give it a few months to see if it fits. Are you making good connections? Stick with it. If not, consider testing a different platform.

Social Media Platform Comparisons

Not all social media sites are created equal. If you've done your homework from Chapter Ten and you have a pretty good idea who your Rachel Reader is, the following stats may help you decide where to spend your time. The Pew Research Center evaluated the demographics of the users of various sites. There is more data available, but here are the basics to get you started.

Site	% of Female users	% of Male users	% Age 18 - 29	% Age 30 - 49	% Age 50 - 64	% Age 65+
Facebook	83%	75%	88%	84%	72%	62%
Instagram	38%	26%	59%	33%	18%	8%
Twitter	25%	24%	36%	23%	21%	10%
LinkedIn	27%	31%	34%	33%	24%	20%
Pinterest	45%	17%	36%	34%	28%	16%

Table: Social Media Statistics[3]

Now that you're armed and dangerous, plan to spend some time on the sites where your potential readers hang out to discover how they use their platform. Here are a few tips:

- Facebook is used for business (fan pages), personal interaction (personal timelines), and to build community (groups). It has the largest user base, and spans the widest age range.
- Instagram is used to share videos and pictures with a community. It's most popular with the younger demographics, high school and college age to thirties.
- Twitter is a news feed used to spread sound bites or marketing links, or gather people around topics or information streams using hashtags. You're limited to

140 characters per post, so keep that in mind as you consider your marketing strategy in Section Four.

- LinkedIn is a professional social networking site used to connect businesses with other businesses, or for career change. It's not commonly used by fiction authors, but nonfiction authors and industry experts can use it to make new connections and find others interested in their topics.
- Pinterest is used to organize articles, pictures, and other kinds of information into boards for personal use (DIY projects`, recipes, travel information), or to share with others. A large percentage of the demographic is moms and housewives.

There are many other social media platforms and each has its strengths and weaknesses. You'll have to do a little research to discover which will work best for you.

Branding Yourself

There are entire books on this topic, but here are a few tips to get you started.

Create a logline. Many corporations have a logline. It tells the consumer something about that company in a simple phrase. It's a mini mission statement. Think Nike—"Just do it". Or Apple—"Think Different". Authors often have loglines too. Clive Cussler is "The Grandmaster of Adventure". John Grisham is "America's Favorite Storyteller".

- If you're reading this, you probably can't make such lofty claims, but there is something distinctive about you and your work. I suggest keeping loglines simple and to the point. Don't try to be too clever, or chances are nobody will get it. My logline is: "Stories of

Domestic Suspense". Someday maybe someone will name me "The Goddess of Suspense", but until that day, I'm keeping my logline humble and to the point.

- Use graphics to create brand recognition. If you're published, or getting close, you have a book cover. If you have a book cover, you have a graphic artist who understands your brand. I recommend contacting this person and having them create headers for your website and social media pages. Colors, fonts, style are all recognizable at a glance. Unless you have an artistic background, it's best to use a professional for this.
- Things to include in your headers are: a terrific headshot, your name and logline, and book covers if you have them.

Beyond the Basics

Different authors have found success in different ways. While it's important to learn what has worked for others and incorporate best practices into your own outreach strategy, it's also important to be the unique individual that you are. Be creative.

Do you love attending conventions? Bring a clipboard and sign people up for your mailing list. Do you write at coffee shops? Leave behind a copy of your book or bookmarks at your favorite locations, better yet, prop up a book in front of your laptop while you're writing. You never know what conversations you'll start.

Chapter 12

Onward: Seeing Beyond Book One

It's often said in author circles that the best way to sell your book is to write the next one. Apparently, there is a magic line crossed somewhere around book three where sales on all your books begin to pick up. It makes sense. The more products you have, the more likely your perfect readers will stumble across you.

There is also another reason to start thinking about the next book; it means you're beginning to think like an author. Our first books are near and dear to our hearts. The process of writing them, seeking publication or planning to publish ourselves is an emotion packed journey. Not only that, but we're waiting with baited breath to see if our creation will be received into the ranks of successful books. We see it as a referendum on our writing ability, our creativity, our potential, and our future.

In other words, we're not objective about our first book. To be honest, we probably won't be completely objective about our second, or our third, or our fiftieth either, but many positive things happen when we write them.

Things That Happen When We Write More Books:

- We become more objective about our work.
- We become better writers.
- We gain insight into our audience.
- We get a bigger vision.
- We have a career.

One book does not a career make. Yes, once it's published you can call yourself an author, but career authors write books. Lots of them. While you're waiting for an agent to say yes to your query, or waiting for the edits from your editor, while you're building your website and creating your marketing funnels, I suggest spending some time every day on the next book.

Singers sing. Dancers dance. Artists paint. And writers write. Don't fall into the trap of thinking that if your first book doesn't get picked up, or doesn't sell well on Amazon, it's a cosmic sign that you should give up. It isn't. It may be a sign you need to take another writing course, or read another book on craft. It may mean there is a heck of a lot of competition out there, and this whole author thing is going to take longer than you thought. Or, it might mean you need to write your next book.

But I don't know what to write, you may be thinking. Let's brainstorm it. My first book was a nonfiction title called *The Wine and Chocolate Workout*. I was working in the health and wellness field at the time, and I wrote it for my clients. I thought I'd said everything I had to say about how to have a healthy life in that book. But had I?

If I'd stayed in that field and wanted to build that particular audience, I could have created a *Wine and Chocolate* series, like the *Chicken Soup for the Soul* series. I could have written a *Wine and Chocolate Workout* for the busy mom, for the runner, for the baby boomer. I could have written a *Wine and Chocolate* recipe book, workbook, or created *Wine and Chocolate* exercise videos.

Genre Jumping:

Writers are readers first. As a reader, you probably enjoy many genres, and that's great. The more widely you read, the more interesting your books will be. However, it isn't always the best strategy from a marketing perspective to write in multiple genres for many reasons.

- It's time intensive to grow an audience. The more genres you write in, the more different reader groups you must appeal to. The people who enjoy your sci-fi novel aren't the target market for your romance series.
- If you write in two or more different genres and use the same author name, you run the risk of confusing your readers. This means employing pen names. For every pen name you use, you must replicate your platform building. Each name should have its own website, mailing list, social media sites, etc . . .

As you can see, genre hopping may scratch your creative itch, but it's time and labor intensive. Once you have a raving fan base, you may be able to segue from one subgenre to a related one. For instance, Nora Roberts writes romance, and romantic suspense, and supernatural stories with strong romantic elements. Not all of her readers will like all three, but they are similar enough to create crossover.

Her murder mysteries are written under a different pen name, J.D.Robb, because they appeal to a different audience. Nora Roberts can do that. She has an entire marketing team at her disposal. She's a superstar. We aren't there yet.

Writing a Series:

Series are very hot in fiction right now because they not only sell books, they help authors build a fanbase. People want to know if they invest time in a story, get attached to the characters, or the world, that there will be more to come. How can you turn your stand-alone novel into a series?

I took a class from Lisa Wells on writing a series and according to her there are four basic types: the really big book, the linked sequential, the linked stand-alone, and the loosely connected stand-alone. Let me explain.

The Really Big Book Series:

An example of the really big book series would be the *Lord of the Rings* trilogy in which book one starts Frodo's story, book two continues it and book three wraps it up. If it wouldn't break your arm to hold, the entire trilogy could be one really, long book.

The Linked Sequential Series:

Jan Karon's *Mitford* series is an example of a linked sequential series. In this kind of series there is an overarching storyline that moves from book to book. If you read them out of order, you will wonder who certain characters are and when so and so got married. But each novel also has a subplot of its own that wraps up at its end.

The Linked Stand-Alone Series:

The linked stand-alone series is the most popular of the mystery or crime genre. Think Agatha Christie's *Miss Marple* books, or Lee Child's *Jack Reacher* series. Each story is complete in itself. They can be read out of order. What links them is the protagonist.

The Loosely Connected Stand-Alone Series:

Finally there are loosely connected stand-alone novels. In these, each story is complete and has its own protagonist. What connects them is the world, and the cast of characters. An example of this kind of series is the Tana French books set in Ireland. All her protagonists work for the Murder Squad. Each story is a separate case, solved by its own detective, but the detectives are connected through the world she has created.

How do you choose which kind of series is right for you? Certain genres lend themselves to certain series types. Fantasy, especially high fantasy, is perfect for the big book because often the author is telling the story of a world, or an epic journey with a huge cast of characters. It's a history of sorts. The linked sequential series is a natural for following a character through the stages of life, or for a family epic. Linked stand-alone novels are a perfect foil for the quirky detective.

I chose to write loosely connected stand-alone novels for my *7 Deadly Sins* series. I like domestic suspense, and by definition domestic suspense occurs when something bizarre happens to Joe Blow Average. The plots generally revolve around the idea that a normal person—not a cop, or an ex-Navy Seal, or a crime reporter—stumbles into a life or death situation.

Since thrillers need to be tight stories with a ticking clock going in the background, neither of the first two types of series made sense. I also couldn't have a real estate agent (the protagonist in book one) bumping into serial killers every other month, so that ruled out the third. There was only one option left.

Take a hard look at your book. Does it have series potential? Is it long enough to divide into three books? Or could it, like Tolkien's *The Hobbit*, be a prequel to a series? Whether you turn your current tome into a series or not, if you're serious about all this author stuff you should start writing your next book.

Section 4

BOOM

"I went for years not finishing anything. Because, of course, when you finish something you can be judged."

—Erica Jong

You've fought the good literary fight, built the foundations of an author platform, and the finish line is in sight. Boom! It's time to publish your book. There are a few things you'll have to take into consideration if you want a successful book launch.

B - Budget

O - Overwhelmed and Overextended?

O - Out There

M - Momentum

The book launch may be the most exhausting, exhilarating, debilitating event of this entire adventure. The aim of this section is to prepare you for take off.

You'll learn how to set a budget and create a marketing plan before you even hit the runway. You'll get some tips about how to present yourself like a pro in public. And, finally, we'll attempt to inspire you to rise above post-publishing melancholy and use the momentum you've built to start your next big adventure.

Chapter 13

Budget

Regardless of whether you're an independent author-preneur or working with a traditional publisher, you're going to have to consider your costs. Yes, the indie method is far more expensive, but even traditional authors have expenses.

Many authors have a fear of numbers, or at least dislike math. Maybe you've never used a spreadsheet. I understand, but I'm here to help you figure it all out. The basics are easy. Trust me.

Ready? The first step is to set yourself up with a blank spreadsheet. I like to use Google Sheets—it's free and fairly self-explanatory. But you could also use Excel or any other spreadsheet software you have access to. I don't recommend a word document, however, even if you add in a table. Dedicated spreadsheet software is much easier.

At the top of the spreadsheet, create five columns: Cost Category, Vendor, Estimated Cost, Amount Paid, and Notes.

Now let's consider your expenses. What is your publisher going to do? What do you have to do? Who are you going to hire? (See Chapters One and Two) How much do they charge? Are you able to trade services?

Here are some examples, for your consideration:

General business expenses:

- Website domain
- Business cards
- Newsletter service

General manuscript preparation:

- Developmental Editor
- Copy Editor
- Proofreader
- Print copies to send to readers/editors
- Postage to send print copies

Book production:

- Cover design
- Formatting
- ISBN purchase (International Standard Book Number—a 10 to 13 digit code number that identifies your book.)
- Paperback proof copies

Marketing:

- Promotional Materials (Bookmarks, postcards, swag, etc.)
- Website design

- Digital imagery (Social media banners, teaser images, etc.)
- Advertising (newsletter promotions like BookBub, Facebook ads, PR assistance, etc.)
- Giveaways (print copies, shipping, digital gifted copies)

Cushion:

- Make sure you pad a little extra money into your budget for surprises. I guarantee there's something you've forgotten or somewhere that you'll go over budget. Prepare for the unexpected.

Once you have all your categories listed, start filling in the vendor names and the estimated costs. At the bottom, create a sum for your total expenses. This is how much money you need to find to start production. Is it higher than you expected? Think through everything again and find places to cut costs. Is it lower than expected? Lucky! I wish I were you!

As you start to hire and pay vendors, fill in the Amount Paid column. Were you able to find savings? Great. Did you go over budget in an area? Where can you make that back?

The notes column is for any exceptions or oddities that occurred during the production phase. Was your cover designer late? Note that. Did the cover designer give you a discount because you booked the covers for your short story prequel and companion novella at the same time? Note that.

A budget is a living document, not a commandment written in stone. Revisit your budget once a week, or at least once a month to make sure things are going as planned. If not, make changes.

We've included template spreadsheets in the appendix as examples for your overall book budget, and for the specific marketing costs you plan to invest in for your launch. Use these templates as a guide when thinking through your own expenses and setting up your own spreadsheets.

A Note on Advertising and Public Relations

The amount of money set aside for advertising varies greatly from author to author. There are many vehicles available to get the word out about your books. They range in cost from free to so pricey you need a full-time salary to afford them. You'll have to decide how much money you want to spend first, then explore the options that fit into your budget.

For example, with my first book I didn't have an advertising budget at all. Instead, I reached out to book bloggers and Amazon reviewers. I asked if they would be interested in a free copy of my book in exchange for an honest review. It was hard work and time consuming. I had to carefully review blogger submission policies, make sure they liked books similar to mine, and then reach out to each blogger individually. But I did it, and I sold a few copies along the way.

When I launched my second book, I had a bit more money to spend, and was looking for an easier, faster way to reach more readers. With that in mind, I focused on paid newsletter mailing lists instead of one-on-one outreach.

BookBub and Baby-BookBub Sites

There are dozens of newsletter advertising sites with large lists of book buyers, often organized by the genres they enjoy. Each day their subscribers receive an email promoting deeply discounted or free e-books. Exposure to these readers can be a game changer for many authors, especially when launching a new book at a discount, or when running a countdown deal or free promotion (see the *More on Kindle Unlimited* section on page 104).

The biggest player in the newsletter advertising game is BookBub, but they're incredibly difficult to get into.

Luckily, there are many smaller companies with the same business model that are easier to access. At the time of this writing, the following are some reputable choices for multiple genres.

- Freebooksy / Bargainbooksy
- eReader News Today (ENT)
- Bookperk
- Reading Deals
- Booktastic
- Riffle
- The Fussy Librarian

In addition to the above, there are many discount book sites that focus on specific genres. Asking other authors in your genre which sites worked well in their recent promotions can be a great way to find new lists to target.

Maximizing Your Promotions

When you run a discount or short-term promotion, you must first set the dates, and then begin your marketing campaign. The goal is to get as many purchases or downloads of your book in that time frame as possible. Of course, you should always market to your own fan base, your email list and your social media followers, but including outside advertising will add to your reach and the effectiveness of your promotion.

When selecting a newsletter advertiser, you'll want to focus on reputable lists with a low cost per subscriber and a targeted audience. Paying ten dollars to reach ten thousand genre-specific readers is more valuable than paying ten dollars to reach twenty-five thousand readers with no genre targeting.

Time your ads to be released during your discount days or Countdown Deal, preferably with an increasing audience size. The largest lists should be emailed at the end of your discount period to maximize your overall ranking before your book returns to full price. That way, if you just break even—or even lose money—during the promotion itself, the elevated ranking will increase your visibility and result in more full-price sales in the days and weeks after the promotion.

This process has been used by many authors to hit bestseller lists. *The Wine and Chocolate Workout*, Greta's first nonfiction title, hit number eight on one Amazon bestseller list, thirteen on another, and made it to the overall Kindle bestseller list at ninety-eight, by discounting it to 99¢ and advertising with two different Bookbub-type companies.

Other Advertising Options

The final thing to consider is paid advertising on Facebook and Amazon. These ads should only be used by experienced authors and advertisers. It's very easy to spend a lot of money with little to no return if you don't know what you're doing. It's beyond the scope of this book to go into detail on these ads, but there are courses and guides that can teach you what you need to know. Check the appendix for further resources.

Chapter 14

Overwhelmed and Overextended

With over three hundred thousand new titles arriving on the U.S. scene every year, how can little 'ole you and me expect our books to be seen, never mind purchased? It's overwhelming. If we had the budget of a major corporation, we might be able to buy our way into a slick advertising campaign, but for most of us, whether we're traditionally published or indie published, that's a pipe dream.

In order to create a manageable marketing plan that stays within our budget, we need to change our mindset. We've been taught that marketing is about manipulating others to put money in our pockets. But here's the truth, it's about putting something into theirs. In other words, generosity sells books.

The internet has enlarged our world. We now reach across the globe for products, services, and information about everything from software glitches to dog training. I buy sun block from China and produce from Mexico. My guess is my grandmother never spoke to anyone residing in India in her entire life. I speak to Indian customer service reps for American companies on a monthly basis.

Joanna Penn, whom I consider one of my early virtual mentors, encouraged me to independently publish my first book, *The Wine and Chocolate Workout*, from Australia, and continues to educate me on the state of the global publishing industry from Bath, England.

The internet has made our world much smaller. It's expanded our reach, but it's also given thousands of people access to our personal lives. People have strong opinions today about politicians and celebrities as well as their neighbors. Opinions they'd have had no ability to form before Facebook and Twitter began broadcasting our every foible and misstep. The internet has put a telescope into our hands, but it's also put us under a microscope.

Entrance or exit, which is it? It depends on which side of the door you're standing. Authors, aspiring or otherwise, are taught they must have an online presence if they hope to sell books. Savvy buyers, we're told, purchase products based on peer reviews, or from individuals they know, like, and trust.

Instead of overwhelming us, this new marketing mindset can be used as a guide for creating our strategy. The myriad of opportunities and internet offers can be shaken through the *know, like, and trust* sifter. Let me give you some examples.

Know: The Costco Marketing Method

Costco is the best (or worst) place to shop when you're hungry. There are food-sampling stations every few isles. I've been known to do lunch on my feet while filling my cart. Sometimes I even go back for seconds and no one slaps my hand.

Why are they giving away so much product? Aren't they worried about overhead? The answer is no, because they understand the first principle of generosity—give me a bite and I just might buy a box.

As a writer, your product is the written word. If you want to entice readers to purchase a volume, give them a sample. There are a number of ways to do this and as you move deeper into the writing community, you'll find more.

The Costco Method, as applied to books:

- Blog on your own site: What better way for people to get to know you than to read your blog.
- Blog on others' sites: Find someone with a similar audience and offer to boost their content.
- Be your authentic self (kind of) on social media: I don't suggest airing your dirty laundry, or even your political persuasion unless it's part of your platform, but otherwise, share away.
- If you have a series, consider giving part away for free: Some authors give away the entire first book, others choose a sample or a short story set in that world. Either way, you're enticing readers and hooking them into your series.

- List your book in Kindle Unlimited on Amazon: Kindle Unlimited is the subscription service for Amazon readers.

More on Kindle Unlimited

If you're pursuing the independent publishing route, there's one big decision you'll have to make before you start planning your marketing: do you want to sell exclusively on Amazon, or do you want to go wide, selling through iBooks, Kobo, Smashwords, etc. in addition to Amazon? There are pros and cons to both routes, and this is a decision unique to each author and each project.

Kindle Direct Publishing (KDP) is the self-publishing platform produced by Amazon. By filling out an online form, uploading your cover and interior files, and hitting submit, you'll have a book available for sale in the Kindle store. While there are many decisions that need to be made on that form, the biggest is whether or not to join KDP Select.

By checking the box for KDP Select, you're agreeing to a 90-day term of e-book exclusivity in the Amazon store. That means, you can't sell your e-book anywhere else. Not iBooks. Not on your own website. Nowhere else but Amazon.

In return for that exclusivity, you gain access to the Kindle Unlimited (KU) subscription pool. Your book will be available to borrow by subscribers, and you'll receive a per-page-read payout from the monthly KU pool of money. You'll also be able to run special pricing promotions on your book: up to seven days "Countdown Deal" (a one to seven day discount on your book to as low as 99¢, maintaining the same 70% royalty rate that Amazon pays on full price books over $2.99) or five days free. These can be powerful promotional tools, especially when combined with advertising (see the *Advertising and Public Relations* section) and newsletter cross-promotions (see the *Building Trust with Other Authors* section).

However, you're obviously losing any and all potential sales on other sites. This is especially painful in the international markets like Canada and Europe, where Kobo holds a big market share. In some countries it's even larger than Amazon's. Plus, many people fear putting their eggs in one basket, and being dependent on one distributor.

Here's the rub: if you only have one book available for sale (ahem . . . so far) then you'll have a really hard time promoting your books on the non-Amazon sites. Sure, you can discount or run a giveaway, but without a series or backlist of other books for readers to buy, there won't be any follow through sales. From personal experience, it's extremely challenging to market a single book without the promotions and KU borrows provided by KDP Select.

However, once you have three or more books available for sale, especially in a series, you begin to have more marketing options on the non-Amazon platforms. You can make your first book in the series free to attract new readers. You can build relationships with the merchandising representatives at the various companies. They make the promotion and advertising decisions for their sites, and they're more likely to talk to you if you have a big backlist and a strong sales history. And you can still run giveaways and promotions to drive sales across all platforms.

But once you go wide, you lose access to the KU borrows. If that's a significant portion of your book income, you won't want to sacrifice it.

One strategy to consider—the one I'm following—is to put your books in KDP Select until you have three or more titles available for sale. Then, once the page-reads drop and sales decline on Amazon (which is inevitable a few months after launch), uncheck the box for automatic renewal of KDP Select, and take the books wide. To me, it's the best of both worlds.

Two Options for Free Sample Delivery

In the modern era of Internet marketing, there are always new products and new platforms that swear to bring in new readers for your books. Many of these platforms fail before they ever truly get started. But there are a couple worth mentioning when you're using the Costco marketing method.

Instafreebie and BookFunnel are two websites that offer easy ways to bring readers onto your mailing list. They each have their strengths and weaknesses, but they've been around long enough that they've established a loyal following.

BookFunnel began as a site where you could upload multiple versions of your book—Kindle, ePub, pdf—and they give you a link to send your readers. You can choose to limit the number of copies that can be downloaded, and there's even a way to keep track of who downloaded specific copies, so you don't have to worry about piracy. They take care of all the customer service, with explicit instructions and troubleshooting to make sure your readers can download the book into the device of their choice. They've recently begun branching out into giveaways in which readers are required to provide their email and sign up for your newsletter in order to download your book, but at the time of this writing, their promotional network is not as strong as Instafreebie's.

Instafreebie is another easy way to distribute your free books. However, their strength is in their reader network. Like BookFunnel, Instafreebie giveaways require the reader to provide their email to download your book. Instafreebie automatically collects those emails and—for most newsletter service providers—will send them directly to your list. No middleman required. But where BookFunnel mostly relies on author promotion of the giveaways, Instafreebie actively promotes the large multi-author giveaways to their own community of readers.

Both of these companies offer easy ways to grow your audience through samples of your work. However, be warned: some readers who use these sites to download free books have no interest in purchasing your books in the future. Many will sign up for your email list to get the book, then immediately unsubscribe or worse, send your emails to their junk inbox and never open them.

It's up to you to implement a strategy to turn these cold readers into true fans, or decide if the free sample method is right for your book business.

Like: The Amanda Palmer Marketing Method

Amanda Palmer is a musician who decided to give her music away for free and ask for support later. It was a bold, gutsy decision that worked for her. Her record label couldn't make a profit with twenty-five thousand album sales, but on her own she brought in over a million dollars from twenty-five thousand fans. How?

The first thing she did was develop rapport with individuals. Then she invited them to download her music for free. Then she asked for financial support from those who could afford it. The individuals became a supportive, vibrant community. I suggest listening to her TEDTalk.

Many authors have followed her lead. They offer Podcasts, or other work without charge and ask for support. Sites like Patreon (https://www.patreon.com/) make it possible for artists, musicians, writers, and other creatives to set up membership communities where people make a minimal monthly donation.

Here are a few ways to increase your "likeability." Again, there are links to more in depth material in the appendix.

Increase your likeability

- Get to know like-minded people on social media and at in-person events.
- Partner with a charity. People respect those who put their money where their mouth is.
- Cross-promote with other authors. There are organizations that will help you do it.
- Celebrate others' successes. Everybody loves a cheerleader.

Trust: The Tenacity Marketing Method

If you or I want to find author success, we're going to have to be generous with our time and talent. More than once. In fact, we'll have to show up and give many, many times over if we want to build a trusting relationship with our readers. In my experience, generosity sells books.

We have to get to a place where the message is more important than the money. A place where we see our readers as real people that we have the privilege to connect with. A place where we applaud others in the writing community because a success for one of us is really a success for all of us. It isn't easy.

Building Trust with Other Authors

I mentioned this briefly in the *Two Options for Free Sample Delivery* section on page 106, but one great way to build trust with readers and reach a new audience is through multi-author cross-promotions—a group of authors agreeing to share each other's work with their own audience. This can be done through a free giveaway page for Instafreebie where all of the involved authors announce the giveaway and provide a link to their audience. It can also be highly successful for new releases and short-term sales.

For example, I participated in a cross-promotion with four other authors in my genre. During the first week of each month, we all agreed to feature a promotion from *one* of the other authors to our list of newsletter subscribers. It took five months for every author to be featured. The deal was the highlight of the newsletter, earning the featured author more visibility. Plus, a newsletter feature demonstrates a certain level of trust and legitimacy—the newsletter owner is essentially saying they endorse this book, and think you, the reader, might like it too.

The key to a multi-author cross-promotion is delivering on your promises. If you want others to share your work, you also have to share theirs. But it's a balancing act. You don't want to share sub-par books with your audience, or you could lose their trust. Done right, you provide value to your readers and to other authors, plus gain access to a new group of readers interested in your genre. It's a win-win for everyone involved.

Chapter 15

Out There

Once upon a time, I was a cog in the corporate wheel working as a consultant for a big accounting firm. Long hours, long commute, and tedious work, but it was immensely educational. One of my biggest lessons had nothing to do with the work itself. It was how to look and act like a professional.

Now that your book is on the market, you're going to have to drag yourself away from the computer and take off your sweats once in awhile. I'm not saying authors should all wear three-piece suits or pencil skirts when they do bookstore readings. But maybe they should if they are a lecturer at a conference. The important thing is that you present yourself in such a way people will be attracted to your words and your work. You want them to take you seriously. Let's look at three different scenarios.

Online: The Virtual You

Whether or not you realize it, you have a virtual identity, and yes, a brand. Your headshot, book covers, social media banners, posts, and shares will determine how people interact with you and your work.

If you're a fiction author and post about politics on your author page, you very well might anger or alienate a segment of your potential readers. You could lose sales. Then again, if you're a nonfiction writer whose books relate to politics, it might help you attract readers.

Your headshot can attract or alienate people as well. Does it reflect how you want the world to see you? Some authors prefer the candid photo, while others prefer the work of a professional photographer. Either way, the photo says something about you, so make sure it's saying what you want it to.

Remember, everything you say or do online is saved in perpetuity. If you slam another author, editor, or agent, even on your personal profile page, it's entirely possible that person will find out days, weeks, months . . . potentially years into the future. Think before you post.

Live and In-Person: Spending Time with Readers and Fans

When it comes to in-person events, audience is key. What do they want to see? How do they expect to interact with you? Readers generally want the experience of getting to know you, whether it's reality, or not. In-person events are a bit like a performance, except you're not only the actor, you're also the director. You get to choose which parts of yourself to share, which personality you want to feature.

"Haha," you say. "I don't have multiple personalities. I'm normal."

First, you're a writer. You're definitely not normal.

Second, do you act the same with your best friend as you do with your boss? How about your parents versus your kids? We all share different parts of ourselves with different people. If we're aware of what we're sharing, we can give our readers the experience they're looking for, without pretending to be something that we're not.

For example, I write tough-girl dark fantasy adventures. When I attend events with readers, I'm not going to wear breezy summer dresses or faded old yoga pants, both of which I feel comfortable in. I'm going to wear black. Maybe with jeans and black boots. When I'm talking to my fans, I don't talk about my kids or my fitness classes, I talk about my books, or fantasy fandoms that we share.

Universal Truths of Personal Presentation:

- Dress nice. That doesn't mean you have to wear your Sunday best, but you shouldn't look like a homeless person or a college student who just rolled out of bed. (Unless maybe you're writing about the homeless, or college students who just rolled out of bed.)
- Smile. Growling at readers will only scare them away. Even horror fans want to feel comfortable approaching their favorite authors.
- Be positive. Don't rant about why your books aren't selling well, or complain about the injustices of the publishing world. Don't moan about the cover that your publisher forced on you, or describe the horrors of trying to format your book in Scrivener. Instead,

focus on the good. They aren't lackluster sales, it's slow-growth. You might not love the image, but you love the typography on the cover. Isn't it fantastic? Stay upbeat and keep your readers engaged to earn your audience.

Professionalism: Networking with Other Writers

When you're working with other writers, you want to present the best parts of your writer self. So, in addition to everything I've said above, there's an added layer of decorum to consider.

First, writers often meet around watering holes, especially at conferences. Social lubrication certainly helps introverts like me overcome the introduction hurdles. If I ever meet you at a conference, wine is my drink of choice—which is, of course, why Greta (author of *The Wine and Chocolate Workout*) and I get along so well.

The bar might be open, but there's water on tap, too. Keep track of what you've had, and trade off for water now and then. You'll thank me later. I can't tell you how many corporate conferences I've attended where individuals embarrassed themselves and then had to deal with the humiliation. Some of these episodes were never forgotten. A few interns even lost their jobs. Don't be that guy (or girl).

Second, deliver on your promises. Did you say you would cross-promote someone's novel in your newsletter? Then do it. Did you agree to review a book? Do it! It doesn't take much to earn a reputation as a flake, or worse, a mooch.

Third, give as much as (or more than) you receive. Whether that's on a *quid pro quo* basis, like trading reviews, or giving back to the writing community by reaching out a hand to pull up the authors behind you, never take without giving something of equal or greater value in return. Karma is real.

Finally, don't be a jerk. This seems like common sense, but seriously, don't be a jerk. People will make you angry, things might not be going your way, but it's harder to rebuild a burned bridge than put out the fire before it starts. Nice guys finish first, remember?

Chapter 16

Momentum

From the days when I was tucked in at night with a bedtime story until the present, literature has played a powerful role in my life. Books and stories transport me, mesmerize me, and make me a different human being. They alter my worldview, sometimes they make me better, sometimes worse, but they always challenge my preconceived notions. Books burn into my solid, made-up-my-mind mentality regularly.

In my early years, Nancy Drew's careful choice of sleuthing outfits made me aware of the importance of dressing for success. In my teens, Shakespeare's wandering forest fairies caused me to ponder man's position in the universe. Poe's secret in the chimney introduced me to insomnia. Peter Benchley's *Jaws* ruined me on ocean swimming.

As an adult, my faith has been broadened more by C.S. Lewis's *The Chronicles of Narnia, The Screwtape Letters,* and *That Hideous Strength* than from any Sunday sermon. (And I've heard some great ones.) Gillian Flynn's *Gone Girl* nailed my view of modern romance with Amy's description of the

"Cool Girl". Living vicariously through stories is a wonderful way to learn and grow without all the pain and angst of life.

Since tackling the fiction writing process, I now know the writers who pen the tales don't have things as easy as their readers. Writing is hard work, and the publishing process is even harder. Writers who put fingers to keyboard and make their mental meanderings, wonder-ings, and what-if-ings public are some of the bravest people around. It's scary to cross the line of normal. Please keep on. I want to read what you think about the universe and elves and end times and healthy eating and dragons and serial killers and the girl next door.

Writers provide the ingredients for the soup of next. If it weren't for Alfred Hitchcock, *The Twilight Zone,* and *Star Trek*, where would we be today? Some of those stories probably paved the way for iPhones, laptops, and *CSI*. I'm sure I heard somewhere Steve Jobs was a Trekkie. What tomorrow brings comes from the minds of today.

To every writer who has to write ten books to find the one that alters thought, I hope you don't let the critics stop you. You will write silly stories that don't cut it. You will write drivel. You will write redundancies. But in the trying, you might write genius. You never know.

You might be the one who inspires an engineer or inventor, politician or preacher, explorer or archaeologist to change the world. Douglas Preston and Lincoln Child (authors of the *Pendergast* series) have had a big impact on me. Neither set out to be the next Tolstoy.

It really isn't about you. It isn't about your success, or your Amazon reviews. It is about the spark your story might ignite. It may take fifteen books before one strikes the match, but once it's struck what fires can be lit? Your mission is much more than pleasing New York publishers and snarky Goodreads reviewers. Your mission is to help others live vicariously.

PUBLISH

We know writing and publishing a book can be an exhausting process. We highly suggest a European vacation, a trip to the beach, or at least a nap when you're done. But after the celebration, we hope we have inspired you to pick yourself up, dust yourself off, and start your next book.

Appendix 1

Publishing Personality Quiz Answer Key

1. How do you manage your personal finances?
   a. I have overdraft protection (A)
   b. I have a detailed budget and monitor revenues and expenses (I)
   c. I balance my bank accounts occasionally (S)
2. What's your ideal production schedule?
   a. More than two books a year. (I)
   b. At least one book every two years. (A)
   c. At least one book a year. (S)
3. How do you envision your role in the editorial process?
   a. I see my editor as a collaborator and want to find mutual agreement. (S)
   b. I value critique but see myself as the final decision maker. (I)
   c. I might not like it, but understand I will have to make changes to see my book in print. (A)

4. How do you feel about marketing?
    a. I want time to experiment and explore the marketing options that best fit me. (I)
    b. I want to work with a team to promote both myself and others. (S)
    c. I want to build my author platform before publication and am willing to promote myself assertively. (A)
5. How willing are you to give up control of your cover design?
    a. Not at all. (I)
    b. Completely. (A)
    c. Would like some input. (S)
6. What kind of financial investment are you ready to make in your work?
    a. I have some money to invest, and am looking for a financial partner. (S)
    b. I don't plan to invest. I want to sell my writing for a set fee. (A)
    c. I'm willing to spend money now with an expectation of a long-term return on investment. (I)

Count the number of times you answered with each letter:

A = Agented Traditional ___________
S = Traditional Small Press ___________
I = Independent ___________

The highest number is the publishing path you are most inclined to follow.

Let us help you succeed in your author career.

Join the OC Writers Membership List!

All new subscribers receive the FREE Pro-Author Packet, including:

- Publishing Personality Quiz
- Publishing Personality Comparison Chart
- Book Production Budget Template
- Submission Tracker Spreadsheet
- Marketing Budget Template

Subscribe Today at http://www.OCWriters.network/publish

APPENDIX 2

SERVICE PROVIDERS AND ONLINE RESOURCES

Service Providers Used in the Creation of this Book:

Kimberly Peticolas
Editor & Interior Formatting
www.KimPeticolas.com

Are you an indie author in need of an editor and publishing guide? Pursuing traditional publication, but looking for extra help to snag the agent of your dreams? What about a small business looking for assistance with publishing projects? Look no further!

Kimberly Peticolas is an experienced editor, writing coach, and publishing consultant working with clients from a variety of backgrounds. No matter your publishing goals, she's here to help you achieve your writing dreams. With a la carte services ranging from one-on-one author coaching to detailed manuscript editing and proofreading, or even extra help to improve your writing skills, Kim has you covered.

Check www.kimpeticolas.com for current rates and available services.

Other Resources

Places to find literary agents or boutique publishers online:

- Agent Query
- Carissa Taylor: Pitch Contest Calendar
- Duotrope
- Jane Friedman - How to find a Literary Agent
- Poets & Writers - Literary Agents Database
- Publishing and Other Forms of Insanity - List of Publishers Open to Author Submissions
- Publisher's Marketplace
- Querytracker
- Savvy Authors
- Writer's Database
- Writer's Market
- Taglines & Queries:
- Flogging the Quill
- Margie Lawson Writer's Academy - Queries that Sell
- Query Shark
- Writers Helping Writers
- Writer's Market

(Also check the agent websites you might be interested in. Many of them have blogs where they talk about what grabs them in a query, and what doesn't.)

Facebook groups for indie authors:

- 20 Books to 50k
- An Alliance of Young Adult Authors
- Indie Authors International

Writing conferences – where to find them:

- Association of Writers and Writing Programs - Conference Database
- New Pages - Writing Conferences and Events
- Writers and Editors - Conferences, Workshops and Other Learning Places

National genre based organizations:

- Historical Writers of America
- Horror Writers of America
- International Thriller Writers
- Mystery Writers of America
- Romance Writers of America
- Science Fiction and Fantasy Writers of America
- Sisters in Crime
- Society of Children's Book Writers and Illustrators

Setting up a website:

- Getting Started with WordPress
- New to WordPress - Where to Start
- Getting Started with SquareSpace
- Getting Started with Wix

Appendix 3

Recommended Reading

Feel like you need to dive a little deeper into one or more of the subjects we covered? Here's a list of books we've read and used in building our own author businesses.

Writing Productivity

- *Take Off Your Pants!: Outline Your Books for Faster, Better Writing*, by Libbie Hawker
- *The Writing Productivity Bundle*, by Monica Leonelle
  Includes: Writer Better, Faster; 8-Minute Writing Habit; and, *Dictate Your Book*
- *The Essential Guide to Getting Your Book Published* by Arielle Eckstut and David Henry Sterry
- *Publishing 101: A First-Time Author's Guide to Getting Published, Marketing and Promoting Your Book, and Building a Successful Career* by Jane Friedman

Query Letters and Traditional Publishing Resources

- *Writer's Market 2018*
- *Guide to Literary Agents 2018*
- *Independent Publishing Resources*
- *10 Step Self-Publishing Bootcamp,* by S.K. Quinn
- *5 Steps to Self-Publishing for Love or Money,* by S.K. Quinn
- *Let's Get Digital*, by David Gaughran
- *Successful Self-Publishing*, by Joanna Penn

Book Marketing

- *Let's Get Visible*, by David Gaughran
- *How to Write a Sizzling Synopsis*, by Bryan Cohen
- *How to Market a Book*, by Joanna Penn
- *Mastering Amazon Ads*, by Brian Meeks
- *Mastering Simple Facebook Ads for Authors: Find Readers and Build Your Mailing List,* by Mark Dawson

Appendix 4

Template Spreadsheets

Digital files in Excel format can be found in the Pro-Author packet, available FREE on www.OCWriters.network/publish.

Book Production Budget - Traditional

This template can be used as a general guide to the types of expenses you might incur as a traditional author. Consider this spreadsheet a starting point: add or substract line-items as necessary. Try to think through all of your expenses before you begin paying vendors, and revisit this budget periodically to make sure you're staying on track.

Category	Item	Vendor	Estimated Cost	Actual Paid	Difference (Estimated - Actual)	Notes
General Business Expenses	Website Domain & Hosting					
	Website Design					
	Newsletter Service					
	Business Cards					
	Total - General Business Expenses		0	0	0	
Manuscript Preparation	Developmental Edit					
	Copy-Edit					
	Total - Manuscript Preparation		0	0	0	
Marketing	Advertising					
	Giveaways					
	Promotional Materials					
	Total - Advertising and Promotion		0	0	0	
Cushion	Cushion					
Total Costs			0	0	0	

Book Production Budget - Independent

This template can be used as a general guide to the types of expenses you might incur as an independent author. Consider this spreadsheet a starting point: add or substract line-items as necessary. Try to think through all of your expenses before you begin paying vendors, and revisit this budget periodically to make sure you're staying on track.

Category	Item	Vendor	Estimated Cost	Actual Paid	Difference (Estimated - Actual)	Notes
General Business Expenses	Website Domain & Hosting					
	Website Design					
	Newsletter Service					
	Business Cards					
	Total - General Business Expenses		0	0	0	
Manuscript Preparation	Developmental Edit					
	Copy-Edit					
	Formatting					
	Proofreader					
	Cover					
	ISBN					
	Proofs					
	Total - Manuscript Preparation		0	0	0	
Marketing	Digital Imagery					
	Advanced Review Copies					
	Advertising					
	Giveaways					
	Promotional Materials					
	Total - Marketing		0	0	0	
Cushion	Cushion					
Total Costs			0	0	0	

Marketing Budget Template

This template provides more detail on the types of marketing expenses you might accrue. You can use the total of each category as a line-item on the Book Production Budget.

Category	Item	Vendor	Estimated Cost	Actual Paid	Difference (Estimated - Actual)	Notes
Digital Imagery	3D Book Covers				0	
	Advertising Images				0	
	Teaser Images				0	
	Total - Digital Imagery		0	0	0	
Advanced Review Copies	eBook				0	
	Paperback				0	
	Total - Advanced Review Copies		0	0	0	
Advertising	Paid Newsletter Promotion				0	
	Facebook Ads				0	
	Amazon Ads				0	
	Total - Advertising		0	0	0	
Giveaways	Paperbacks				0	
	Postage				0	
	Gift Cards				0	
	Gifted eBooks				0	
	Total - Giveaways		0	0	0	
Promotional Materials	Bookmarks				0	
	Postcards				0	
	Other "Swag"				0	
	Total - Promotional Materials		0	0	0	
Total Marketing Expenses			0	0	0	

Submission Tracker

This spreadsheet can be used to track your query letter subm ssions, review requests, or other requests for information. We suggest using a separate spreadsheet for each type of submission. For example, if you're querying multiple projects, you'll want a separate spreadsheet for each manuscript.

Agent/Editor Name	Company Name	Email Address	What Did You Send?	Date Sent	Time Frame	Response Date	Response	Notes	Follow up
Amelia Agent	Hard to Impress Agency	Amelia@HTIAgency	Query Letter & 10 Pages	8/18/18	6 months (or forget it)	10/10/18	Send Full!!!	She loved it. Will let me know about full by 1/30/19	

REFERENCES

1 Issac, Brad. "Jerry Seinfeld's Productivity Secret." Lifehacker. July 24, 2007. Accessed August 07, 2017. http://lifehacker.com/281626/jerry-seinfelds-productivity-secret.

2 Ciotti, Gregory. "5 Scientific Ways to Build Habits That Stick." 99U by Behance. March 09, 2016. Accessed August 07, 2017. http://99u.com/articles/17123/5-scientific-ways-to-build-habits-that-stick.

3 Friedman, Jane. "A Definition of Author Platform." Jane Friedman. January 03, 2017. Accessed August 07, 2017. https://janefriedman.com/author-platform-definition/.

4 Greenwood, Shannon, Andrew Perrin, and Maeve Duggan. "Social Media Update 2016." Pew Research Center: Internet, Science & Tech. November 11, 2016. Accessed August 07, 2017. http://www.pewinternet.org/2016/11/11/social-media-update-2016/.

About the Authors

Greta Boris

Greta Boris is the author of *A Margin of Lust, The Scent of Wrath*, and *The Sanctity of Sloth*, the first three books in *The 7 Deadly Sins*—a series of taut psychological thrillers that expose the dark side of sunny Southern California.

Her nonfiction work includes the Amazon Bestseller *The Wine and Chocolate Workout - Sip, Savor, and Strengthen for a Healthier Life*. She's also the Director of O.C. Writers, a community of over 1000 published and aspiring authors in Orange County, California.

You can visit her at http://gretaboris.com. She describes her work (and her life) as an O.C. housewife meets Dante's Inferno.

Megan Haskell

Megan Haskell is the award-winning author of the Amazon bestselling dark fantasy adventure series, *The Sanyare Chronicles*. The first book in the series, *Sanyare: The Last Descendant*, won the Readers' Favorite Bronze award and was honored with a B.R.A.G. Medallion for quality in independent literature. She lives in Orange County, California with her husband, two young daughters, and one ridiculously energetic dog. You can find her on her website at http://www.MeganHaskell.com.

OC Writers

Read Greta and Megan's blog for writers at http://OCWriters.network/blog

Greta and Megan are the directors of a free community of over 1000 published and aspiring authors in Southern California, but writers from anywhere in the world are welcome to participate. O.C. Writers is a hub of encouragement, information and resources for writers in every phase of their publishing careers. Join us today at http://OCWriters.network and on Facebook at https://www.facebook.com/groups/OCWriters/.

CPSIA information can be obtained
at www.ICGtesting.com
Printed in the USA
FSHW020731200719
60217FS

9 780999 435427